Song of Myself:

A Korean-American Life

Song of Myself:

A Korean-American Life

— A Memoir By —

Yearn Hong Choi

Poetic Matrix Press

Front cover art, *To A Star* by Euna Park.

ISBN: 978-0-9824276-8-2

Poetic Matrix Press
www.poeticmatrix.com

To My Wife, Bong Hee Kim,
who has been sharing my life,
both ups and downs.

Contents

Signaling Walt Whitman

by Ellen Olmstead, Professor of English,
Montgomery College, Rockville, Maryland

Although Yearn Choi identifies himself as an ordinary man, his has been a remarkable life...the odyssey of a Korean in America. Naturally, because it is a memoir, this book explores the theme of identity. What does life on the hyphen (Korean-American) mean for his generation versus his children's generation? Yet the author's journey intersects with the trajectory of this country in the midst of struggle and transformation. What is America? Choi lived, studied, and worked in the Pacific Northwest, the Midwest, the Deep South, and the nation's capital over four decades, while the U.S. was in the throes of the civil rights, anti-war, anti-nuclear, and environmental movements. As activist and political scientist, he problematizes the simple binaries of black and white and of American and Asian.

What does democracy mean in the U.S. and in South Korea? What is the American Dream? Choi shifts perspectives to capture his sense of being an outsider as an "Asian immigrant with an accent" in America and of an insider as a principal organizer of the nascent Korean-American community and its institutions. Within this multi-genre memoir that blends critical and romantic notes, he deftly weaves poetry, philosophy and political science, history and sociocultural commentary, and slices of life that read like short fiction revolving around unforgettable characters and celebrities.

Artful, informative, heartfelt, provocative, and always engaging, Choi's memoir will prove an invaluable and unique contribution to American and Asian Studies by a seminal poet and incisive scholar. With *Song of Myself:*, Yearn Hong Choi immediately signals Walt Whitman. Yet he rivals Whitman in style and exceeds Whitman in scope.

Introduction

"In all people I see myself ..."

Walt Whitman
"Song of Myself," 1855.

Song of Myself:

A Korean-American Life

The Orientals were inscrutable! They are still inscrutable. I want to present my "inscrutable" life to America with this book. This is a song of myself. This is my life as a Korean-American from the first moment I landed in Seattle on May 30, 1968, to today.

When I look back on my life in America, I think first of the great events I was witness to. I particularly think of the political protest movements, which I believe show the greatness of America. The years of protest against the Vietnam War, the civil rights movement and the rise of environmental protection — each in its own way showed the strength and openness of this new country. A turbulent era put the United States' creative minds and energy on full display. Lately, I have experienced a kind of déjà vu watching Barack Obama's candidacy and victory in the 2008 presidential election. It is an exhilarating time all over again. Can America return itself to true greatness?

When I look back on my life here, I also think of the personal honors I had as a scholar, a poet, a government official and a political writer. Each, it seems, was tempered by an unexpected personal trial. I came to this country with a few hundred dollars and ended up a college professor — a great honor. But my tenure evaluation at one university offered the first real sadness in my life, when I was denied tenure. I was a victim of racial discrimination, I concluded — I was denied even though my qualifications were equal to or better than those of my peers. There was ample evidence that the school disliked the "overrepresentation" of foreign faculty. And so they denied me. Others, wrongly I thought, claimed it was "my accent." This was the first time I ever saw my own limitations. I came to know them, and confront

them with humility — a growing experience. Around the same time I was happy to become father of two children and to watch one become a fine young man and the other a fine young woman — an even greater growing experience.

I also think of my honors. One was becoming a high-level government bureaucrat-scholar in the Office of the Secretary of Defense. Imagine that — a foreign-born naturalized citizen who gets to work for the Secretary of Defense! My position was assistant for environmental quality. In that position, I also felt frustration, though of a different sort. I expended much energy, and looked with much hope, on the subject of radioactive waste management. I believed in the capacity of this country to solve pressing environmental problems surrounding such dangerous materials. But the 1980 and 1982 radioactive waste management acts the U.S. Congress passed have not made much progress even today, after more than 20 years. This showed me that America has its own limits. We need nuclear energy, nuclear research and nuclear medicine, but we don't care much about properly handling the waste generated from nuclear activities. Every time, the vagaries of the federal system conspire to stop reasonable agreements. My own view is that nuclear arms should be banned — but the waste from producing the existing nuclear weapons can and should be safely disposed of for good, since the activities that produce it are so vital. It never happens.

The record of inter-state compacts and cooperation in the search for a safe, secure and permanent low-level radioactive waste disposal site has been shameful. The Founding Fathers intended inter-state compacts and cooperation to be the basic foundation of the federal system of government in the United States of America. But here it has simply failed.

I also think of Washington, which has been my home. I think of how the Korean-American community here has blossomed. In the 1980s our community was very small. Today, Korean-Americans are both numerous and prosperous in the Washington area, particularly in Annandale and Centerville, Virginia. It wasn't always this way. In the early 1980s, those of us who were here were not many but we were politically active and socially engaged. In 1981, I was a charter member of the Korean-American church for South Korea's democratization movement. I met and helped exiled South Korean politicians including South Korea's famous former president and Noble Prize winner Kim Dae-jung, among others. In 1990, I created the Korean-American Poets and Writers Group, and in 2000, I created the Korean-American Poetry Group. During those years, I read my poetry in the Library of Congress in 1994 and 2003, and published poetry books in Korean and in English.

Next I think of how my freedom to travel to my home country was not allowed and, if I ventured out, would have been dangerous, due to my political activities and writings. I lost my father in 1982 when a sudden heart attack took his life. It was a shock to me. My father's funeral left me with no choice but to get my U.S. passport quickly and to take the chance that I could be arrested and imprisoned by South Korea's authoritarian regime. The funeral struck in me a fear of seeing my dead father, plus the added fear of what a repressive government might do to me.

In 1996, after South Korea's political liberalization, I had the chance to teach at the University of Seoul as a visiting professor, which I accepted. I was glad for the opportunity to see my family regularly for the first time in decades. I soon found that I could not leave my aging mother after a couple of years. My mother had Parkinson's disease. So I remained in Seoul. But to do that, the University of Seoul asked me to give up my U.S. citizenship in exchange for my professorship. So, I ended up reluctantly renouncing my U.S. citizenship so that I could be present for my mother. I lost her in 2004 but not before being able to stand beside her in her last seven years.

When I retired from my teaching career in 2006, I returned to Washington, where my wife remained while I lived in Seoul. I felt guilty to her for my long absence from home. I also felt guilty to the United States for what I considered a betrayal even though the circumstances put me in a difficult bind not of my own making. Then, this country's good graces worked for me yet again. My wife made a petition for my Green card and, after two years of waiting, I received it. I am grateful to the United States.

I enjoy walking into the woods every morning, and reading and writing after walking. I am grateful for the life I have been given. I

play golf with my friends once or twice a week. Life is still going strong. My heart is still as young as it was in my twenties.

I enjoy a retiree's life and its comforts, even though poets and writers typically do not get that chance. I get the best of both worlds. This is my blessed life. I have been fortunate to place my articles in the *Los Angeles Times*, the *Washington Post*, the *Washington Times*, the *Virginian-Pilot*, the *Ledger-Star*, the *Indianapolis Star*, the *Daily Press*, the *Clarion-Ledger*, the *Roll Call*, the *Japan Times*, the *Korea Times*, the *Korea Herald*, the *Korean Quarterly*, and the *Korea Monitor*. I will continue to write my song of my life.

I am not a famous person. I am an ordinary first-generation Korean-American, an immigrant who first arrived here as a foreign student in 1968 and made his way over four wonderful decades.

"In all people I see myself," wrote Walt Whitman in the famous "Song of Myself." I quote him here for the simple reason that we can learn from one another — we learn from the stories of ordinary people, not just the rich and famous. Our stories are worth hearing. I am part of a very reticent generation of Korean-Americans.

I came to this country with a few hundred dollars in my pocket. I earned a doctorate at Indiana University, taught at four American universities, married my beautiful wife, raised my two beautiful and successful children, served in the United States government, wrote poetry and published Op-Eds in newspapers around the world as we grappled with the big political and social issues of the day. I watched the universities as they were rocked by war and protest in the 1960s. I met famous American poets and writers and activists. I watched, and played a small role, as environmentalism blossomed in the 1970s and 1980s. I learned as America struggled with the intractable problems of race. I taught you, you young Americans, and I taught your parents.

We, Korean-Americans, work and strive but we mostly keep quiet about ourselves, about our lives. This is to our children's detriment, to our nation's and to our own. We are not well known in the United States — perhaps, in some respects, not even to ourselves or to our children. I have been surprised watching my son and daughter, nieces and nephews as they read my reminiscences. It is as if they are meeting me for the first time. That is, they are meeting the father, uncle or friend

as he views himself — and we grow closer. They learn new things about themselves.

My story is about values. It is about learning these values, scrutinizing them, upholding them, passing them on, and sometimes rejecting them. But what are values — What are Asian values? American values? Family values? I wrote an essay, "Asian Values Meet Western Realities," for the *Los Angeles Times* on September 7, 1999.

The concept of Asian values has puzzled me. I am an Asian man. I was born and raised in Korea and came to the United States in 1968. I later became an American citizen. I have a Korean wife, and we have two children. Who am I? Korean or American? Korean-American is the simple answer. But I still have an identity crisis even after 40-some years in the United States as a college professor and a U.S. government bureaucrat.

Asian values are easily identifiable from a personal perspective. My two children sought and got jobs in New York City. I would congratulate them under normal circumstances, but I did not. I wanted them to find jobs near home in the Virginia area, because their mother would be alone as I left for Seoul to care for my own mother and they left for New York City. My wife was left all by herself.

When I moved back to Seoul to take care of my aging mother, I was fulfilling my role as a man of Asian values. This is often called "filial piety." My children are young college graduates steeped in American values. Career advancement and development are prime concerns for them. I had hoped that at least one of them would have chosen to stay at home to take care of their mother. They understood my reasoning, but rejected it. They feel their mother was still young and a working woman. They could comfort her with visits, by e-mail and telephone calls, they argued.

My daughter explained her situation to me this way: "Dad, you came to the United States for your advanced study at Indiana University. You left your parents. I am in the same situation." But I told her, "My parents were young then. Your mother is not young any more. She is in her 50s."

Are they good children of filial piety? Or are they a mixture of Asian and American values?

In a sense, my wife accepted her children's career growth in New York City. She took care of her children before she took care of her husband. I cherish my wife's Asian values based on filial piety and her motherly devotion to her children, and, I have to admit it, I detest my two children's American values. Where is the protection for family? They did not care what their parents wanted. Individualism prevails over family values.

Asian values can be defined in many ways. Authoritarianism and Confucianism, the two major components of the Asian value system, are hierarchical, whereas democracy, egalitarianism and individualism are the major components of the American value system. However, though they may be unpopular here in America, I can see the virtue of my Asian values — of taking care of my aging mother. And, I would simply point out, is this value really "Asian" in the first place? It is part of the Ten Commandments after all. Honor your father and your mother.

After much pondering, I can see a very basic reason why the Asian reality is so different from the American. At least part of it has to do with the way modern Western society has caused other forces to step into what used to be the place of the family. Aging parents in the United States are taken care of by a third party (nursing homes and Uncle Sam). In Asia, aging parents are taken care of by their children. The Asian reality will probably be gradually changed when the wealth of Asian nations increases to American levels, if citizens opt for the same arrangements. Then, perhaps, nursing homes and government welfare programs will take care of aging Asian parents, too. This, at least, offers a "big picture" explanation.

Thinking about these basic differences allows me to view the subject in more shades than just black and white. Maybe our family's separation has nothing to do with Asian or American values. My children's spirit of independence and career development would not contradict family values after all — in their eyes this is certainly true — insofar as society continues to look out for the elderly, just in a very different way than the one I am accustomed to. My children still believe that they honor and love their parents, although they are apart from us. I may never quite view it in the same way. But at least I can come to understand their point of view.

Perhaps some day we will truly live in a global village, at which point we can live peacefully in a sea of community. Then, there would be no need for scholarly debates on Asian, American and family values. Until then, though, our values differ and it matters to talk about them.

As you can see, the discussion of these issues is not necessarily exclusive to the "Asian" in America. Something similar afflicts most others Americans also. It is for that reason that I think my story is relevant to people who are not of Korean ancestry. I would even say that in some senses this story is about ordinary Americans. I watched America grow up. I saw what the country looks like from the view of an outsider, but I also crossed that line. I'm an American, too. Where and when I crossed this line, I can't quite say. I watched this country's history unfold and became a part of it.

If I were to summarize everything I've learned, it might go something like this. As an immigrant, I know that the opportunities my adopted country afforded me outweigh what was often a confusing and solitary experience of a "New American" caught between worlds. Working my way through school and as a young professor, I learned the importance of hard work and fairness but also the role of sheer luck. I experienced what injustice and prejudice felt like. I know first-hand what a fair and just government is worth and what it means not to have such a government, as was the case in Korea before it turned to democracy. I know what an attack on democratic government looks like.

I saw many Americans give kindly of themselves to strangers — people to whom they owed nothing. It left me in awe with a sense that I knew one secret that explained why America was great.

I also know the value of poetry and feeling: I am at heart a romantic, a poet who would have thought that the life of an itinerant — contrary to my father's wishes — would have been quite suitable. I know the Korean-American dilemma: My "filial piety," as it is called, my family values often conflict with the modern lives we undertake with their fast-paced careers and constantly changing social mores. In the end, I am a believer in a just and humane society. It takes much effort to keep things just and fair.

This, then, is the humble record of one first-generation Korean immigrant's life. The immigrant's life can be lonely, divided between two cultures. I hope this memoir will be a meaningful and valuable contribution to Korean-American history and literature. I hope it will show other Americans a thing or two about who we are, building a bridge between Korean-Americans and their neighbors. Most often, the Korean people are "inscrutable." We can bridge the gap between East and West — we have to.

For today's young Korean-Americans: It is time to bridge our own gap. There is such a large distance between first-generation Korean immigrants and their children. There is always an island, or maybe a whole continent, between one man and another. This book is about getting one man over to the other.

Let us all be from somewhere.
Let us tell each other everything we can.
Peace on Earth.

CHAPTER 1

Seattle, My First Port-of-Call

The fight for liberty, and against corruption, is a powerful draw to young students everywhere. So it was for me as a student at Yonsei University in Seoul in the early 1960s. I had a strong sense of justice. But like many similarly minded people of my generation, I found my outlet in a new field in the college curriculum: public administration. My field's first great advocate, Woodrow Wilson, the United States' 28th President, captured many of the ideals that attracted me. While serving as a professor and later as President of Princeton University, Wilson argued in the late 19th and early 20th centuries that administration is the most vital function of government; fortunately for me, and I would submit for democracies around the world, he convinced a great many people. This was the beginning of the Progressive Era. Figures such as Wilson were reacting to the dirty, ugly dominance of corruption in American politics at the time: the bad years of Tammany Hall, the boss politics in New York, Chicago, Boston and elsewhere, the political machines that corrupted and the crushing influence of corporate monopolies of the era. It all struck a chord.

I came to learn this history by heart because, at the time, I saw much of the same in my own country. Korean politics was also dirty and ugly in the 1960s. Of course, one important difference from Wilson's America of the early 1900s was that government had become the single largest industry, by far, in Korea in the 1960s. Another was the repression: We did not have the open system of government that propelled Wilson and the reformers to power. For these reasons, I thought, Wilson's insights were even more valuable to Korea than they were to his contemporaries.

It was a dilemma. Korea needed good, strong and accountable government badly. We were a poor country. The nation was still recovering from the devastation of the Korean War and World War

II. Economic development was the foremost goal. Government activism in the economy had been the norm since the 1950s under the guidance of American planners, but it surged under Army General Park Chung-hee after Park orchestrated a successful coup d'etat in 1961. A government's active intervention in the service of national development was well and good in my opinion — indeed it was vital and necessary for a poor country like Korea. But the repression was a different matter.

Park quickly installed himself as the head of what would become an authoritarian regime. He ruled the country through his party cadre, a politicized military headed by himself, the KCIA — Korean Central Intelligence Agency, modeled after America's — and a government bureaucracy intimately linked to these Park-aligned institutions. As a young man, I felt the Second Korean Republic under Prime Minister Chang Myon (known as "John Chang" to Americans) was, for all its troubles, legitimate and capable enough of governing. The trouble was that some far-left and leftist-progressive political forces made the government unstable. They were simply too radical for most Koreans, opening a window of opportunity for Park's coup d'etat. So the general struck.

Park made his case to the Korean people for the coup on grounds of national security, development and independence. It resonated with a great many. Not for me. Sure enough, when I left Korea in 1967, the nation was advancing economically under his 5-year economic development plan. The worst of the corruption was yet to come, and what was already present was not very visible to the public. The government was stable and fostered growth — that much is certain.

But today everyone acknowledges what was missing. There was no accountability, no democracy and plenty of opportunity for rank corruption. Park was an American ally, but this ally's domestic politics diverged greatly from that of the United States and from the ideals of democratic accountability that I held dear. Generally credited with spurring the incredible economic advances in the nation of my birth, the Park regime was one of the many repressive Cold War governments that the United States backed for reasons of anti-communism. Student leaders, labor leaders and dissidents were thrown in jail. There was no opposition, at least no opposition capable of exercising genuine influence. The permanent ruling coalition sat atop government much like Wilson's corrupt nemeses in Tammany Hall and other complacent political machines in early 20th century America. It engendered a mode of cronyism in politics and business. The yearning for something better drew me to my field of study where those higher ideals that so struck a chord in me were found.

* * * * *

I was born to a Confucian middle-class family. My parents, school teachers both, graduated from the best high schools in the era of Japanese colonial education, a period during which education was prized. Teachers were venerated; they held a high social status reserved in America today for college professors, and often not even there. After my mother married, she quit teaching to raise a family (I am one of five). My father, meanwhile, eventually joined the governing administration of the First Republic under President Syngman Rhee in the 1940s. He was a high-level political appointee in the government's Planning Office in Seoul, which is something like the White House's Office of Management and Budget. But his job eventually ended after a series of irreconcilable conflicts with Rhee's autocratic leadership.

By 1950, as was common for many families, the Korean War uprooted us. We were forced to move to Pusan, at the southernmost tip of the Korean peninsula. During the South's dimmest days early in the war, North Korean forces had so overrun the country that all but a few hundred square miles of territory around Pusan were in Communist hands. Backed by American forces, in just a few short months the South pushed back to reclaim all of what is now South Korea and pushed well into the North. The war festered in a bloody, destructive stalemate until the July 1953 armistice that created the Demilitarized Zone along the 38th parallel, which continues to divide the two Koreas to this day.

After the war I returned to Seoul as a middle school student, but my family stayed in Taejon, near my father's home in central South Korea. My father was unemployed for a period owing to his conflicts

with the government. So, my grandparents' farm provided for our basic needs such as grains and vegetables. My grandmother on my mother's side was still managing the farm at that time! By Korean standards we had a middle-class life. In a country where the per-capita income was less than $100 during the 1960s, we were fortunate.

Before long I was off to college. I became a member of the first class of public administration graduates at Yonsei, Korea's oldest university, with roots in the late 19th and early 20th centuries. My classmates included a great many public-minded people who went on to influence Korean politics and society over the years including a Cabinet minister, the governor of Kyunggi Province and a number of college professors. It was a stimulating time to be at Yonsei. I graduated in 1963 and subsequently entered upon military service for two years, just like all able-bodied Korean males then and now, as required by law. I was a member of the first class of ROTC-commissioned second lieutenants in the Army of the Republic of Korea. Among my duties: I was an interpreting officer between the Korean army and the United States Army in Korea. I was a public information officer, as well as an assistant to the Korean Army's Corps of Engineers. One year of my service was spent in the front line near the DMZ, and another was spent at the Second Army Corps headquarters in Taegu. We say "front line" even in what was ostensibly peacetime because the threat of war was constant. To this day, there is no peace treaty between the two Koreas. Skirmishes along the border, though rare, happen every few years even to this day.

Once I completed my service, I returned to Yonsei to attend graduate school, earning a master's degree in public administration. After this I spent a year in the Philippines as a Southeast Asia Treaty Organization scholar at the University of the Philippines Graduate School of Public Administration in 1967-68. Knowing that I had a special passion for my field and knowing that, to the extent possible, I wanted to see the world, my teachers advised me to undertake advanced study in the United States.

As a young poet and a budding scholar, I was eager to hear their recommendation. I wanted to see the United States. This vast country, with so much presence in my native land, stretched from the Atlantic to the Pacific. America was one of the most admired, and most admirable nations on the entire Earth. I liked American democracy, American literature, and Hollywood movies. It was an open society. I wanted to see this great country: The American people's pursuit of happiness, the free market economy, the Protestant ethic, New York's Manhattan and the New York Yankees, Iowa farms, the Grand Canyon, Hollywood, and Disneyland — the whole thing. I have seen them, experienced them and touched them. Now, I am living as part of America in the so-called post-September 11 tension. I feel this is still a great nation. Its openness and its people's pursuit of happiness have made this nation great. A common man's pursuit of happiness is most striking to my eyes. The United States was thought of around the world as a dynamic country. New ideas and thoughts are proposed and experimented. I began my search for a university with excitement and trepidation.

I ended up applying to the University of Washington in the Pacific Northwest and Indiana University in the heartland. Both held solid reputations in the field of public administration. Both were home to famous scholars in my field. I was pleased with the idea of living in each place, as well: Seattle, the Pacific Northwest with its coastline, moderate climate and closeness to Korea, and Indiana, near the heart of the American breadbasket, where the Mecca of comparative administration was to be found. I was accepted to both universities.

I had the fight for liberty, and against corruption, just as Wilson had, high on my mind.

Seattle is a beautiful city in the Pacific Northwest. It is often the first port-of-call for new arrivals to the United States by way of the Orient. The very name of the city is beautiful to my eyes and ears. The University of Washington in Seattle is the oldest public university on the West Coast, and it sits on the shores of the Union and Portage Bays. It was attractive for a young poet and social scientist — waves and seagulls were perfect, I thought, when a person needs a break from thinking and studying. I was also keenly aware how often the sea has served as a setting in many great American literary works. From Herman Melville to Ernest Hemingway to John Steinbeck, a young man (or woman) who appreciates great literature appreciates the ocean.

* * * * *

Initially, though, I had intended San Francisco as my first port-of-call. I left Manila for San Francisco in 1968 by sea, by way of the now-defunct American President cruise lines. These trans-Pacific cruise ships would take a few weeks to ferry passengers across the Pacific Ocean. These few weeks of travel, it might surprise younger readers, were considered very much the norm, the common mode of transportation before mass air travel (the carrier, American President Lines, would permanently suspend the service five years later, in 1973). When the ship anchored at Yokohama, Japan, I had a detour. I called my uncle who lived at that time in Chiba, a city northeast of Tokyo. He told me to get off the ship and take a taxi from Yokohama to his home in Chiba. When I arrived, he suggested that I stay for a week at his home, which I did. I was surprised when he purchased a Northwest Airline ticket for me from Tokyo to Seattle — an expensive rarity in those days before mass air travel. That was how I made my way to Seattle.

For me, this was a lesson in family matters. My uncle supported my voyage because I was the first person in the Choi clan to head to the United States. Even though Japan was a wealthier nation than Korea, and my uncle's circumstances were also relatively favorable, it was extremely expensive for him to do. I still remember his generous heart to me. My uncle, a small businessman, emphasized the fact that I was the eldest grandson of the Choi family tree. He wished the successful completion of my advanced studies, as a matter of family accomplishment, loyalty and honor.

Naturally, my uncle was concerned about my financial situation. Back then, my poverty was nothing shameful. The nation was poor. South Korea's per capita income was only around $70. Such it was after devastating wars and, before that, a colonial history and a record of underdevelopment. I told my uncle that I could earn money from my summer work in Seattle, and start school in the fall semester. I made my promise.

The United States was the land of opportunity. It is one of the few wealthy nations where poor foreign students can earn money and study at the same time if they work hard and are shrewd with

their actions. Was! Perhaps I should say — was. Things have changed. But back then, I accepted the challenge.

Of course, inside the airplane, I discovered how scared I was. There were unknown hardships I was bound to face in this unknown land. I could not sleep, not for a moment, inside the airplane. I remembered at that point the French writer and aviator Antoine De Saint-Exupery and his novel *Night Flight.* Exupery, who fought with the Free French in World War II, drew upon personal experience to dramatize aviation. He himself would vanish over the Marseilles Coast in 1944 in a final mission to collect intelligence on German troop movements. His words resonated within me: "Growth accompanies pain, and you should overcome fear. Fear is part of life."

I believed in youthful and poetic wayfarers in the dreamful land, the vast land for New Frontiers. Now, I thought, I was one of the New Frontiersmen exploring the new terrain. I also remembered in the night-flying the 1955 Hollywood film *Picnic*, which I saw in a Korean theater. The memory of this film — a sort of snapshot of the American Midwest of the 1950s — struck me. William Holden plays an ex-college football star, now a drifter, who falls for a beautiful woman played by Kim Novak in a small Kansas town. She is already spoken for. The "drifter" possibility struck déjà vu in the darkness of the Northwest airplane. If worse came to worst, I would wander the vast land as a young poet, and then return to my home country. It would be my privilege to see the most powerful and prosperous nation on Earth. Not bad for a worst-case scenario. This, of course, is not how things would turn out for me.

* * * * *

On the airplane, by chance, I met a young American man who would end up being instrumental to my first weeks getting settled in the United States. He was the passenger sitting next to me. It pains me to this day that I cannot recall his name, and thus I couldn't possibly know how to begin the process of finding him to say thank you. Here's how it occurred.

As we were chatting, I told the young man that I was going to America to complete my advanced studies. When I told him how little money I had, I remember him sympathetically expressing, "$500

is not a sizeable amount of money." In reality, even that was more than I might have expected to bring, since, at that time, the maximum a Korean was allowed by law to take outside the country was $300. He went on to say that he has a good friend whose house was close to the University of Washington; this friend would be picking him up from the airport. It was pure luck.

I asked him, "Have you seen the film, *Picnic?*" Fancying myself to be like William Holden in the movie, I too planned to hitchhike from the airport to the downtown area. When I told him this, he laughed. "Mr. Choi, you must know it is a Hollywood movie. You are going to face reality. If everyone is hitchhiking, how can the taxicab drivers survive in the United States?"

I smiled.

* * * * *

We landed in Seattle in the early morning. I went through immigration, and, as was to be expected, it took more time for me than for regular American passengers. But my American friend waited patiently.

After my papers were processed, he introduced me to his friend, who was waiting for him at the airport. We went to a downtown hotel together enroute to his friend's house in Seattle. As we did all this, I saw the downtown for the first time — and, to my shock, it was nearly empty. I asked him, "Is Seattle an empty city?" He answered, "Today is Memorial Day. It is a national holiday!" It was May 30th, 1968, Memorial Day.

Memorial Day was and is therefore the most unforgettable day for me. He, a young man in his thirties, offered to let me stay my first night in America in his house near the University of Washington. I happily accepted his hospitality. When we arrived, his wife greeted me after she heard my story from her husband. The young couple warmly welcomed and wished me luck in my American adventure. They had one room for a guest, and I became an unexpected guest in their home.

* * * * *

After I had a nap, I went outside the house. By afternoon, University Avenue, or "the Avenue," was full of hippies, showing their long hair and beggarly appearance and anti-war protest signs. It was quite an extraordinary sight for me. There was nothing like it in Korea. The Beatles music roared from radios, rocking the Avenue under the May sunshine. Some of them were half-nude. It seemed like a different universe from the staid upbringing everyone in Korea had in my generation.

I was anxious to see where my future was, so I walked slowly toward the university. Everything was intriguing to my eyes. The university was clean and neat. The water in Lake Washington was seemingly part of the university. There were not many students out that day, as it was also a university holiday. It was beautiful.

In the early evening before sunset, I returned to the house. My hosts prepared dinner. During the meal, they asked me why I chose the University of Washington over the many fine universities in the United States. I explained my reasoning: "The University of Washington is located in Seattle, one of the most attractive cities on the Pacific Coast and the closest port-of-call to my home country. I want to be near to my home country while I am studying in the United States." They understood my not-so-rational mind. It was a sentimental explanation, but it was true. They guessed correctly that I was a poet. It also happens that the University of Washington was known as a good school for Asian Studies in the United States, so they would expect (and they would be right to expect) that there was a larger-than-average community of Koreans.

My second choice of a university, I told them, was Indiana University. This school was the Mecca of what was called "Comparative Public Administration, or "Development Administration," and this field was of particular interest to me. It was the discipline of famous professors — famous in our field — such as Fred Riggs, William Siffin and Alfred Diamant. Together, they formed the "Group of Comparative Administration" in the 1960s, a cadre of new, forward-thinking and exciting scholars who were watched closely in the developing world, especially in my home country of Korea. My choice of Indiana was based on Siffin and the other professors who essentially built a new academic discipline inside Public Administration. I had read

Siffin's books and articles during my graduate work at Yonsei University in Seoul, Korea. I revered him, and sought eagerly to learn under his guidance.

The following morning, my hosts went to work, and I went to the University with a suitcase and a portable typewriter. I said "goodbye" to my first Samaritans. It was a tearful good bye. I was very fortunate to meet them all and I will never forget them. I wish I could find them even now. I hope this book can locate them. Unfortunately, I don't remember their names. It is painful not to retrieve their last name and first names.

* * * * *

In the morning, the University was already familiar to me, because of my visit the day before. I went to the Office of Foreign Students to meet the director for the first time. It went disastrously. It went so poorly because I made the wrong confession to him: "I don't have enough money for the tuition, and I have to work for the summer months. Please help me!"

His response was immediate and bold. "Your admission is nullified!" he said. I'll never forget his precise words and his tone. He could not believe what I was asking him. "Mr. Choi, how can you study, when you are worrying about where your next meal is coming from?"

In truth, I had falsely reported my financial situation. I wanted to get in, and so I did what it took. On the application form, I wrote something like, "My parents will fully support my advanced study in the University of Washington." Of course, this was not strictly true. We were not an exceedingly wealthy family. So, it made sense that he was angry with me. But consider my position. If I had not filed this false financial report, then I probably would not have received admission to the university. To this day, I am glad, very glad, about my little white lie that caused so much stress that day and for weeks afterward.

My poverty was quite typical. As a matter of fact, my parents even sold a house my grandmother left for me for my study in the United States. They gave me $1,000. It was big money for them, or for anyone in South Korea, but it was not big money in the United

States. I was disappointed by the director's cold decision-making. I could not stay in his office long. His decision was final.

I then went to Gowen Hall, home of the department of East Asian languages and literature, political science and law, society and justice. There I met a Korean faculty member who was teaching Korean literature, Professor D.S. Suh. After listening to my story, he called a Korean student and asked him to help me. A doctorate student in the field of political geography, he picked me up in an hour and took me to a rental house. I met the landlord and paid one month's rent in advance, $100. Here I at least had a short-term plan and a respite. Foreign students and one Canadian gardener rented from the landlord. We shared a kitchen and a bathroom.

Here's something that amazed me at the time. After I received a key for the room, the Korean student, Kim Hyun-kil, drove me to the Social Security Office. In less than 30 minutes, a Social Security officer handed me my Social Security Number and a card with my printed number. I did not know anything about a Social Security number before then, but those numbers have been inseparable from me ever since. Mr. Hyunkil Harry Kim then told me, "I have done all I can. You need your Social Security number before you start your summer work. Now, you can search for a job downtown! Mr. Choi, this town is basically Boeing and the University of Washington. There is a small downtown and there is a small China Town in it. Maybe you can get work there." He gave me a cool response — he clearly must have encountered new arrivals like me regularly, and didn't have much time for my type — but I appreciated his help.

He gave me a ride back to my rented room and dropped me off in front of my new rented rooming house. I got out of his car. He left, and I was all alone in this vast land. From then on, I had to sort out my life on my own.

By coincidence, I met the same man accidentally in June 2007 in a Korean restaurant in Annandale, Virginia. Forty years passed since our first encounter. I had not seen him since. Dr. Kim was working for the U.S. Department of Housing and Urban Development in Washington, D.C. I still hope to meet the American couple who provided the first night shelter in America in Seattle.

* * * * *

As time moves on, like anyone my memories have tended to fade over time. But I can never forget my first night in Seattle and Mr. Kim's care of a poor Korean student who just arrived in Seattle. My social security-card and my first American shelter might strike a reader as not very much, but they were so significant to me. They were acquired from his help. I approached him in the restaurant, quickly learning that he had forgotten all about me. But I remembered him.

With them, I have one more person to record here whom I met in the post office in Seattle. After I settled in a new house, I wrote a long letter to my parents in Seoul and another to my uncle in Chiba, Japan. After I placed the proper stamps on the two letters, I approached the postal worker with my poor English to ask how long these letters would spend in the mail. "How long do these letters reach Korea and Japan?" I asked. The man could not understand my poor English. He ignored me. Then, the man behind me spoke up. The worker's behavior was completely unacceptable and insulting, my linemate said. He asked the worker for his name. I did not fully understand what was going on at the time. I hurriedly left the post office, confused and, of course, ashamed. This was yet another good Samaritan! I could not say even thanks to him. He was compassionate to a total stranger from a foreign country. To this day, I still believe that what makes the United States great are the many average men and women who show sympathy and compassion to the underprivileged, seeking justice and fairness on their behalf.

After this I found a bus heading from University Way to downtown. Soon, I had a job offer from a less-than-fancy hotel, the Roosevelt. The job was nothing like the typical hotel bellman or attendant or manager, however. The job took place in the basement. The offer came suddenly as I was filling an employment form in the personnel office. The official asked whether I was a union member. "I am not," I replied — and he promptly turned me down. At this moment a middle-aged white woman visiting the office asked me whether I could work at the basement for her. I had no idea what for, but I answered yes. I didn't mind. I was relieved. I knew that I was not in a position to say no.

My summer job was to be her personal assistant as she made mugs and ceramics in the furnace. She supplied all of the materials — mud, enamel paints, and tools. She designed the mugs, dishes, flower vases and other goods for her own use and for sale. I enjoyed it truth be told. In the beginning, I made careless mistakes that resulted in the products being tossed into the trashcan. It was a delicate task to mix the mud and water, as I learned, to paint the enamel on the surface, to bake the ceramics at the proper temperature, and to do it all at the proper hours. She was generous toward my mistakes in the beginning. After the first week, my products were all good, and she was satisfied with my performance.

She and her husband lived on the 12th floor of the hotel. She asked me to deliver their meals from the hotel restaurant to their floor. Whenever I delivered their food, her husband gave me a couple of dollars and sometimes $5 for my tip. I appreciated that very generous gesture, since I truly needed the extra income. She was thinking of my earnings that summer.

A Canadian gardener, my next-door neighbor in the rooming house, asked me to work for him on some weekends. He had a truck full of tools. I worked as his assistant, so I could add some money into my summer treasury. All this meant that my revenue was growing steadily, but I also kept my expenditures to a bare minimum. I needed to. I took yet another job at night. It was a dishwashing job in a Greek restaurant on the other side of downtown. Working from 6 to 12 at night at the Greek Village was taxing. I only lasted about one month. It was at that point that I could no longer handle my health. I felt a danger sign from my body when I began vomiting blood from my mouth on the way to my rooming house in the night. I never quite figured out what afflicted me. I had a very sore throat, and the blood. It must have been the stress.

So my Greek employment was short-lived. A dancer in the Greek restaurant regretted my departure from the restaurant. She was looking for me after I left, the manager told me when I visited the restaurant to pick up my last paycheck. She was surprised to know that a poor Korean dishwasher knew Plato and Aristotle, and Greek myths. She admired me. During my short coffee break, I talked to her about the Korean traditional dance under the Fall

Harvest moon, which was similar to the Greek dance style of forming in a circle. It was always interesting to know the common cultural similarities across national boundaries. The Greek people gathered at the restaurant and enjoyed their own ethnic dance, food and drink in the night. I could certainly appreciate that. There was no Korean community of any size or influence at that time. "Korea Town" in Los Angeles, San Francisco or elsewhere was still a decade or two into the future. Seattle had a Chinatown. That, of course, was of little use to me as a Korean, much as some well-intentioned Americans might have directed me there.

* * * * *

This is how it went for the rest of the summer in Seattle. With my savings from June, July, and August, I could now pay my fall semester tuition. When I had one thousand dollars in the savings account, I was finally happy and relieved. So I spent part of the month of August relaxing and visiting the University Library and East Asian Studies Library during the weekend. I read periodicals in the field of political science, public administration, and Asian studies. Once in a while, I also read poems and short stories in the literature section. No one asked me to present my student identification at the Library. I enjoyed the atmosphere of the university during the weekend. The Quad, the name most people called the area of the Liberal Arts Quadrangle, was beautiful with Yoshino cherry trees transplanted there several years before. It was a dream come true.

On the weekends, I would often visit my friend Mr. Soo-Young Auh, one of my Yonsei University classmates who was attending the University of Washington. He was kind enough to invite me to his apartment. His wife was working in a flower shop, providing what we called "a wife's scholarship" for her husband. She was generous to me. Her cooking talent was unforgettable, too.

To my great joy, I found a Korean restaurant on University Avenue. The owners of the restaurant came to the United States for their children's education and training in music. They were the parents of the famous Chung musical geniuses. Pianist and conductor Myung Hoon Chung and his two sisters Myung Hwa Chung and Kyung Hwa Chung, famed cellist and violinist, were known widely. I visited the Korean restaurant and of course ordered the least expensive Bibimbop. I was happy simply to listen to the parents' story of their children's musical talents and achievements. I should admit, though, that, in fine 20th century American form, my main restaurant was McDonald's. I enjoyed fast food for breakfast, lunch and dinner. It was easy, highly economical and — I'll say it — it tasted good.

My summer at this point was a dream come true. I survived my first summer in Seattle. I started it all alone in the Northwest airplane with great fear of my trip to America. But it worked out incredibly well! I was satisfied with my laboring life in the summer and the fall semester tuition in my savings account. So, yes, it was a dream come true.

But it was not a dream that would unfold for much longer in Seattle. Recall that the University of Washington had nullified my admission, and it would not change its mind. So, as I prepared for the fall semester, I made a decision to head to Indiana. Indiana University was the only school I could attend now that "U-Dub" had nullified my admission.

* * * * *

In the last week of August, I left for Bloomington, Indiana. I managed to get a plane ticket to Bloomington via Chicago. I left Seattle grateful to the people I met there, good Samaritans and friends. I was happy. The United States was great, I can recall thinking quite vividly. A foreign student could start with labor and earn one semester's tuition with one summer's work. That is much less possible today, of course.

In 1993, *Sleepless in Seattle* struck a personal note of meaning for me when it became a famous movie. Its lyrics were unforgettable:

Make someone happy,
Make just one someone happy.
And you will be happy, too.

In my first Seattle stay, I met several people who were compassionate to me. I cannot forget them. I am grateful to them, and will be forever. When I look back, Seattle is a beautiful city.

15

I don't know whether I would be able to meet such a friend and helpful couple in Seattle or elsewhere now. Times have changed dramatically. Crime started to prevent hitch-hiking a long time ago and it has never returned. Meanwhile, South Korea has become one of the world's affluent nations, and the United States has stopped being so generous with work permits for newly arrived foreign students. Indeed it is downright stingy. The 1960s now seems to be ancient history.

Here is the poem I wrote about it years later, published in *PoetsWest* in 2007.

Seattle

The Pacific Ocean comes to the inland and makes a city an island.
Winter means rain, not snow, to the city people.
Needle leaf trees contrast with the snow-covered mountain tops
  like the Alps.
The city still has the Space Needle, which was erected
  for the commemoration of the 1962 World Fair, Boeing, and
  the University of Washington.
But I see a Korean young man working as a janitor
  at the Roosevelt Hotel in the daytime
And as a dishwasher in the Greek Village,
  a downtown restaurant at night.
He worked all summer months of 1968
  and went to Indiana University
  after earning one semester's tuition at the end of that summer.
He returned to the town after his retirement
  from a long college teaching career
And checked into the Roosevelt hotel on Pine St. and 6th St.
No one recognizes or greets him.

He was trying to find the house of a young couple
  who accommodated his first night in America on May 30, 1968,
  but failed to find it.

Seattle, My First Port-of-Call

He remembers this city as the place where a couple warmly welcomed
* him, a poor young Korean man who came to town with small*
* money and ambition in his pocket.*
He may come back to the town again in order to find them
* when they are no longer a young couple.*

He falls into the depth of deep sorrow in the un-seasonal autumn rain.

Let us all be from somewhere.
Let us tell each other everything we can.

CHAPTER 2

Stand-by

So off I flew to Chicago from the Seattle-Tacoma Airport. Just three months previously, I had flown from Tokyo to Seattle with a fear of the new and uncertain world I was about to encounter. But as it turns out, I was very happy with my three months in Seattle. What do I mean? Well, at minimum I made enough money to pay for the fall semester's tuition. I survived. Not only did I survive, but I managed to pave the way for my first months in the American academy. This was my primary goal and I managed to attain it. A great freedom this seemed to me!

As the airplane took off and I settled into my seat, I reached once again for something familiar. This time I started to re-read the letters my parents had sent me. There were two letters from my father and mother, you see, I had been keeping in my pocket. They became my talismans. You might even say that they had become guardians of sorts for my life. In one letter, my father wrote: "Son, there is always a green hill wherever you go!" To which I would respond: "Yes, father, I will find the green hills wherever I go!"

In this case, the "guardian" was playing the stern role I had come to expect. My promise to find the green hills was as much an order to myself as it was a promise to him. He had been the one to whisper in my ears, "Son, you should not come back to this airport without a doctorate degree from the United States!" It was my father's wish and stern order. A college professorship was what I wanted; I couldn't fall short. So, I should earn my doctorate, the basic requirement, and then take whatever steps necessary to achieve the goal of securing my professorship.

I never doubted my ability to earn the doctoral degree itself. But my father's whispers were a kind of cold shock to my ears, which did not make me happy in the slightest. I might have preferred a gentler approach, something short of the "ultimatum" that my father's words implied. *Succeed, or else disappoint your father.*

In the worst-case scenario, I would have been happy to consider a year or more of travels in the most prosperous nation on Earth to be a worthy end in itself, if nothing else were to work out. I continue to view the experience — perhaps I am too romantic — of being a wanderer, or a wayfarer, or a poet meaningful and valuable. Needless to say, I am not my father! He was a Spartan soldier through and through.

My father might best be described as a Confucian traditionalist and perfectionist. I was a softer person — I might even say a tearful person. My father did not tolerate my tears, even when I was a young child. He loved his children in his own way. But I did not like the high expectations.

My mother, though, was different. I'd call her an Athenian poetess in contrast to my almost martial father. My mother's letter would prompt tears in me: "I was standing at the observation post, even long after the airplane was out of sight!" she wrote. She said she prayed for my health, safety and success at the observation post at the Kimpo airport long after my plane was out of the sky over Korea.

* * * * *

Four hours later, the plane landed at Chicago's O'Hare airport and I soon found myself walking a long distance inside the airport to reach the smaller terminal for connecting flights. I thought I had a ticket to board the smaller plane flying to Bloomington, Indiana, but, as it turned out, I had a stand-by ticket. The plane was scheduled to leave for Bloomington at three. So I had to wait for four hours in the airport to take that plane.

But, naturally, though I didn't know at the time, I could not fly because the plane was full. I hurriedly came out of the airport heading to downtown Chicago, to the Greyhound Station. I was amazed at the darkening city of tall buildings which I saw for just a few hours then. The bus heading to Indianapolis would depart at 8 o'clock at night. So, I waited, feeling myself suddenly alone in the incredible, large, bustling crowd that Chicago seemed to me to be. I bought the ticket and headed for the closest coffee shop, where I had a cup of joe and two donuts to calm my nerves.

It was a long journey from Chicago to Indianapolis, through many small towns and some hamlets, finally reaching the destination at about 2:30 in the morning. I wasn't finished, of course. I had to wait for another hour to take another bus for Bloomington. At 4:30, I finally landed inside Bloomington city limits. Fortunately, there was a taxicab waiting at that hour. I took it to the residence of a close friend from Yonsei University, Mr. Yong Moon Park, who had a scholarship at Indiana. Soon the taxi pulled up to his apartment on Third Street.

It was a house of many rooms. I could not find my friend's room. So I had no option, I thought, but to wait for the dawn. So I stood around in the darkness of the porch of this two-story house, awkwardly. Before long, though, I discovered that my friend's room was approachable from the back door. I went in and woke him. Young Moon could not believe that I had arrived at such a strange hour of the morning. I was supposed to have arrived the previous afternoon. Since I asked him before I left Seattle to arrange a room for me, he was able to bring me over to the house where a couple of Korean students lived, on the same street, where I would be calling home. These two fellows had a house of two rooms, so I shared one room with one of them.

And that is how I learned the meaning of the term "stand-by."

It's funny to relate it now, but words have a way of tricking the new arrival to the United States. "Stand-by" had a meaning, or so I thought: I could take that airplane standing — like a person who stands in a bus. I did not have a seat, but I had a "stand-by" ticket.

When I explained this to my new roommates I got a good bellow of laughter from them that early morning. From that moment forward, they called me "Stand-by" always. This was my nickname for four years in Bloomington; I never lived it down. But, I did not complain. I just smiled when they called me "Stand-by", a name I had earned learning its meaning the hard way. It's easy in a way to go along with a nickname in a language that is not one's own. Even after 50 years, I don't regard English as my mother tongue, and indeed I'm not completely comfortable in the language even after all this time.

CHAPTER 3

The First Registration Fiasco

Everyone remembers his or her first few days or hours or minutes on campus; it is a time of transition. The senses are heightened. So it was for me. I remember it vividly. After a few hours sleep, I headed over to the campus of Indiana University to see it for the first time with my own eyes.

Even back then it was a huge campus, home to 30,000 students. Bloomington was in some respects a quaint college town. A ten minutes' walk would bring me to the corner of the university grounds. Practically next door was the Greek House Row. Once I arrived, I took it all in for the first time. The campus was beautiful and full of young students in the last week of August.

I passed the woods, old stone buildings, a small church, the Jordan River, a small wooden bridge, Woodburn Hall, the University Fountain, and the University Auditorium, seeing for the first time what I would soon recognize as the school's signal landmarks. Woodburn Hall was the building for the Political Science Department. I went into the building, walking up to the second and the third floors. I was scheduled to visit my faculty advisor the next morning and, not wanting to chance things, I made sure I knew where to go.

I made a mess of it anyhow. The next morning, I returned to Woodburn Hall at 9:20. My appointment was scheduled at 9:00. I was embarrassed.

Mrs. Elinor Ostrom, the faculty advisor, and her husband would later become famous professors at Indiana University, well known for their contributions to public choice theory. At the time they were already gaining some renown. Ostrom had just earned her Ph.D. at UCLA only three years earlier but was well on her way to becoming a department fixture (she is still at Indiana, in fact, as the Arthur F. Bentley Professor of Political Science). I read their co-authored articles in the scholarly journals with appreciation.

As to be expected, she was not happy with my late arrival. I begged her pardon. It happened because I failed to take the same path to Woodburn Hall as I took the day before, and so I got lost. I did not know where I made a wrong turn, but a wrong turn I made, and so I was late. Ostrom could not understand me at all. She seemed to regard me as an undesirable new foreign student — actually, scratch the "seem." She did not like me at all. I didn't know what to say to her, other than "Sorry! I lost myself on the way to the Woodburn Hall." She seemingly couldn't believe it. My excuse was just another excuse in her eyes.

She advised me to take one or two English courses in the first semester, and discouraged me from taking the advanced course I wanted, "Comparative Administration." I told her that I did not have time to take an English course — that I came to Indiana University to get underway in my discipline, to take classes under Professor William J. Siffin who was scheduled to teach "Comparative Administration," and that I could postpone English classes. Siffin, after all, was the person who attracted me to Indiana University in the first place and it would not be possible to postpone his course to the second semester. I registered the courses I wanted to take in the following day despite the adviser's recommendation.

* * * * *

The fall semester went by very quickly. At the end of the semester, my academic performance was a fiasco. The biggest problem was one I never anticipated: I earned an "F" in the English course I did not register for nor attend. The "F" could have been fatal to my graduate work at Indiana University; it was a serious problem. I immediately headed over to protest the grade at the Office of Records. Failing in my first attempts to convince anyone to remove the "F" grade, I was forced to request Professor Siffin's intervention. My professor sent a memorandum to the Office of the Records that eventually forced the removal of the F grade. I survived.

I didn't have the money to take the English course in any event. It was not a required course for a political science degree; I could learn everything on my own, I figured. The 3 credit hours cost $250 — a very large sum for me. I had been striving to save my money and time. I could learn English from everyday life in the United States instead of in a classroom setting, I thought.

Every time after our first meeting, my faculty adviser never acknowledged me in Woodburn Hall or anywhere else I happened to meet her. I greeted her anyway, whenever and wherever I saw her. "How are you, Mrs. Elinor Ostrom!" She hid her anger whenever she saw me. It almost seemed as though she was frightened to see me; I regretted that part.

So, my first meeting with my adviser was one small though serious "disaster" — but I survived it anyhow. That was the one and only serious encounter I had with her during my four years stay in Bloomington, and my only serious difficulty. Being thought of as just another undesirable foreign student who denied the value of faculty advising was a problem I could handle.

A misunderstanding: That's what it boiled down to. Part of it owed to my poor English; part owed to my unwillingness to take that course. But, really, part of it was completely out of my control. Professor Ostrom was displeased with the great many foreign students who, in her view, flouted faculty advising and stood outside the principles she attempted to uphold. Nothing could be further from the truth in my case — as my subsequent academic career illustrated. But, she did not know it at the time.

This was a great lesson for me in the import of misunderstandings in a person's life. Sometimes the facts don't rule. Perceptions matter, even though they're often wrong. For that reason I missed out on a good relationship with an excellent faculty member.

In the fall of 2009, Professor Elinor Ostrom was awarded the Nobel Prize in Economic Sciences, the first woman to receive the honor since it was created four decades ago. She was recognized for her groundbreaking scholarship in "common pool resources," and the idea that fish stocks, water basins, woods, lakes, and grazing land could be successfully managed by the very groups who use them without government regulation or privatization. Her work is a sharp riposte to the long-held belief known as the "tragedy of the commons," the idea that individuals managing shared resources will ultimately destroy them. She has been a scholar in pursuit of "rational decision-making." I wish I meet her happily when I visit Bloomington.

CHAPTER 4

Political Science

As in so many other areas of American life, the 1960s were a period of upheaval and transition in political science, not to mention university life generally. When I applied for admission, Indiana University boasted a Government Department. By the time I arrived, the department's name had changed to Political Science. This was part of a broader transformation of the discipline from a cousin of the humanities to a more empirical, data-driven field of study. I was not entirely comfortable with the transformation.

Public administration, as a part of political science, was one of the battlefields of change. The School of Public Administration was a completely new school founded before I left Indiana University in 1972. Many colleges and universities had a Political Science Department, but some had Public Administration departments inside their Schools of Management. So, unsurprisingly, as a discipline with one foot in an older humanistic sphere of academia, a second in the new social science and with close ties to management, we stood at the boundary of several currents of academic thought. We were part of many of the new changes then afoot.

The Department of Government, though, was unique in Indiana University. It was as much a "Department for Governmental Studies" as anything that might fall under "Political Science" today. Truth be told, even though the name "Political Science" was more common among the colleges and universities, I liked the sound and meaning of "Department of Government." I took to pondering why, since it would seem to the outsider to be somewhat arbitrary. I ultimately concluded that I simply did not like — indeed, was doubtful of — the "science" part of political science.

Coming from Korea and seeing what I had seen, I came to the conclusion that there simply is not very much that is scientific about politics. Much of political life is arbitrary; oftentimes, momentous decisions are made for little or no reason. Certainly that was true of many closed political systems. But, as we were learning, it is also surprisingly often the case regarding open, democratic systems with checks and balances.

None of this is to say that I did not appreciate, nor that I do not appreciate today, the value of a scientific approach toward political affairs. But I had my doubts as to what, among the most important aspects of our field, could be reduced to scientifically verifiable and factually testable hypotheses, which are the hallmark of a "science." It seemed that politics often enough happens due to the will of powerful individuals, their decision-making habits and inclinations, and other hard-to-quantify factors. For this reason I preferred "Government" or perhaps "political studies" to "political science." It reflected my belief that politics itself is more "art" than "science" and that the study of this art is itself subject to the same limitations.

Now, the name change did not change the curriculum in any appreciable manner. The curriculum was designed for those who wished to study the relationship between the people and the government, the people's input or lack thereof in the activities of their government ("input," we called it), and the government's services and activities for or on behalf of the people ("output").

The input-output model was one of the many paradigms of governmental analysis under study in the late 1960s and 1970s. It was "normative," or based on certain premises, in this case a theory of reciprocity in government that had a distinctly modern, economical sensibility. "Demand" required "support"; inputs resulted in outputs. For example, people could demand law and order to result in the protection of their lives and their pursuits of happiness but they would have to finance it somehow. They demand national security, social security, and personal security from their government. To some degree, these principles would be self-reinforcing. Economic order would maintain stability and progress to afford a better life for the people. But, none of this is free.

The government, under this very American model, would consist of the president, congressmen and senators, bureaucrats, and judges. These actors would make decisions to provide national security, social security and personal security and happiness for the people. The people would elect them via periodic elections.

Of course, the elected officials would need to be wise and fair for the system to work. The non-elected bureaucrats and judges would also need to be wise and fair. It quickly becomes evident how often these propositions do not hold in practice.

* * * * *

I had a strong belief back then, as I continue to believe today, that the government should provide personal security to individual citizens, from protection of their lives to adequate protection of their right to engage in the pursuit of happiness. Personal security exists when a person has a stable job, adequate income in light of the government's monetary and fiscal policy, all supported by a proper government manpower policy and regulatory policy.

Good government means democratic government. However, many governments in developing nations, including my country at the time, could not provide adequate services to the people because these nations were so poor. Ineffective governmental leaders and bureaucrats were not able to free the nation from its poverty.

As a young man from a developing nation, I simply did not see very much of the scientific side of political science. I could see only dirty politics. However, I did see the axiomatic truth: economically advanced nations could provide adequate services to the people; higher literacy rates meant higher levels of democratic government; and political stability would bring economic stability and development in a virtuous, self-reinforcing cycle.

Political science can be distinguished from public administration. But can't administration be a science? What is the difference? Generally, I came to believe that the word "political" means something public, making the two close relatives starting with the first half of their names. Science is an object of study, e.g., natural science. It is knowledge covering general truths or the operation of general laws especially as obtained and tested through the scientific method. Scientific approaches or methods are desirable toward political or governmental affairs. Some political scientists have been attempting to make political science a natural science. It cannot be an exact science, though. I never expected to see an exact science developed from voting behavior to presidential decision-making, and indeed this has not come about in the forty years I've been in the field.

Administration is different, though. I would view administration as the act or process of administering the government or non-government organizations. Administration is, can, and should be science.

I found both the "art" and the "science" aspects to have their own virtues. In the first semester, I took Political Science 1 — a "normative" course — and Political Science 2, which was quantitative. PS 1 was an exposure to political philosophy from Plato to Rousseau, Locke, and Hobbes, Thomas Jefferson, and Karl Marx — the "canon," it would be called today. PS 2 was an introduction to basic statistics and statistical analysis of political phenomena from voting behavior to congressional roll calls.

PS 2 was a new course to me. I never took a statistics course in my undergraduate college days in Seoul, and had never seen a computer before I came to Indiana University. At that time, well before Microsoft or Apple became household names, the personal computer had not yet emerged. So, I punched computer cards and submitted them to the computer center's printers. When I made an error in punching a card, the print out would not be available. I would spend all day finding the punching error. This early computing experience was a series of frustrations.

From the questions of political philosophers, I liked to formulate a hypothesis and test it with modern empirical data. Empirical data should be quantitative or quantifiable. Converting the normative political question into a quantifiable hypothesis was a meaningful task I learned from Indiana University in the first semester. I tried to bridge the normative approach and the quantitative approach toward political phenomena. Political history offers many potential quantifiable data. For example, political stability is a normative concept, but the number of political assassinations, military coup d'etats, and violent demonstrations are quantifiable indicators of political stability and instability.

* * * * *

Political science, as one can tell from the above, is a very broad field. Administration is an art, science and process. Poetry and literature can be helpful in the quest to understand political behavior. As a poet, I tried to formulate an hypothesis from *Lord of the Flies, Animal Farm,* and *1984*, three classic political novels, that human nature could be evil — that I could negate one of the new liberal views on human nature that percolated to the surface often in the field during the 1960s. Much of the new commentary in the 1960s seemed to presume the inherent perfectibility of humankind, and the basic goodness of our nature. What if it simply wasn't true? Or, what if it was true, but, in social and political circumstances, these underlying natures subsided to something darker? Certainly there was enough evidence in our century for doubt.

In my paper for PS 1, I argued that the inherently positive "nature of man," a new emerging concept in the field of public administration, was a notion that one who takes William Golding's *Lord of the Flies* seriously would doubt. An optimistic view on human nature, the prevailing view in the field of administration in the 1960s, is a worldview very different from the one proffered in *Lord of the Flies* or the works of George Orwell. These writers maintained an appreciation for the tragic, for the darker side of human social and political existence. Our field would be stronger, I thought, if it accounted for tendencies that these timeless writers had identified. Maybe mankind's nature is not all bad, I surmised. But it was wrong to assume inherent benevolence as we went about planning and developing a science of proper government management.

My PS 1 teacher, Alfred Diamant, appreciated my presence in his classroom. He was a famous scholar on European politics, especially on French politics, who hailed originally from Vienna, Austria. He was warm to me, even though he was a tough man. He was trained by the U.S. Army Rangers and participated in World War II.

In PS 2, the statistically oriented course, I struggled. My paper was good enough to earn an A-, but my in-house exam testing statistical analysis in political phenomena earned an unacceptably low C+. My final course grade was B. All things considered, I was happy with the grade.

In the paper, I tried to test the hypothesis of measuring political stability and instability with the number of political violence, riots, demonstrations and coups, in developing nations in the 1960s, and the relationship of political stability with economic stability and development. Per capita income and the progress rate of economic development were indicators of economic stability and development.

The level of political stability and the level of economic development were positively proven by my data. I did an analysis of coefficient correlations of the two factors, political stability and economic development, for the paper. My teacher, Leroy Rieselbach, was a scholar on American congressional politics who had published a series of well-received books on congressmen and senators' voting behaviors.

John Gillespie, a young professor, taught me statistical analysis using the computer. He died at a young age from heart attack. I read of his death in the American Political Science Association obituary news during my first teaching job at Wisconsin, 1972-73, and was shocked. I missed the man who enjoyed coffee and donuts in the student lounge every morning. American teachers were very close to their students. Students used their professor's first name. Language makes the teacher-student relationship more egalitarian. In Korea, such a relationship was not possible. I felt always some distance between the students and their teachers with veneration.

There's an important lesson in the tension between art and science in political science. The lesson is that both art and science matter. Economics is generally regarded as the "dismal science" for its seeming indifference to "normative" questions of human welfare. But political science also has its "dismal" angle. In some ways, it is even more dismal: The study of war, statecraft and governing must account for all regimes, democratic and repressive. It must seek out, identify and study what is "effective" for efficacy's sake in addition to what is humane and just. For that reason, I am glad that the "art versus science" debate continues to rage, because the art of political science affords us more room for value judgments. It lets us identify what we consider to be noble, praiseworthy, and just in human society, and study them for their own sake. The lesson is that science and art are both useful to the advancement of mankind's quality of life. This has always been the case, and always will be.

At the end of the first semester, I felt as though my eyes were opened. It was an exciting time for me: My professional awakening, a time of much learning and a time when I needed development of my basic career skills.

Then, before I knew it, Christmas was right around the corner.

CHAPTER 5

My First Chirstmas

My first Christmas in Bloomington, Indiana, in 1968 was unforgettable. Professor Siffin, my professional idol before I arrived and even more so after, invited me to his home on Christmas Eve for an experience that I, as an outsider, remember fondly and honor. The evening was warm and cozy by the burning logs of the fireplace. I truly felt a part of American academia by that point, but this Christmas, perhaps to an extent Professor Siffin could not have fully understood, touched me personally and reinforced a conviction of mine. American greatness comes from the kindness of its best to people who are owed nothing.

As you can surely guess, I felt privileged to be part of Professor Siffin's family's Christmas gathering. This Harvard-educated, distinguished professor who had created the new academic field of comparative public administration and public policy didn't have to take in a person such as myself. I was just a foreign student finishing my first semester at the university while working in a local pizza house at night.

He knew this, and he knew the burdens on a foreign student laboring in a pizza kitchen while pursuing an advanced degree. I credit him for not showing his sympathy in the classroom because of this, however. He treated me equally with my classmates in all assignments. Each week we had to produce a book review during the fall semester. Many students complained about the heavy assignments. He then reduced the assignments from all 14 weeks to 10. Wanting to distinguish myself, however, I made sure to produce all 14 assignments without missing a single one.

On Christmas Eve, first Professor Siffin introduced me to his wife, an artist, and his children. What an honor to meet my teacher's wife, Catherine, their two sons, and their daughter!

After the good dinner and pumpkin pie for dessert, my professor drove me back to the boarding house. As I got out of his car, he said to me, "Mr. Choi, Merry Christmas to you! Life is zestful. You should enjoy and appreciate your precious life!" Each word became a shining star in the dark blue sky of the night. Since that Christmas, I have embraced a new Christmas and a new life. How fortunate I was!

* * * * *

Professor Siffin was genuinely concerned not only about my academic excellence, but also about my home country's development. He comparatively studied and analyzed the process of development and modernization of developing nations in the 1960s as an academic in the university, and worked for the US Agency for International Development as director during his leave of absence from the university. So, naturally, my home country was a kind of case study for a professor in his position. It would be an exemplar of sorts of what development economists and social scientists thought possible.

Korea was a poor nation in the 1960s, became a developing nation in the 1970s, and then an industrialized nation in the 1980s. Korea "made it." Back in 1968 Professor Siffin argued for emphasis on a developing nation's desire to change and the national leadership's willingness to enact the necessary changes to build a traditional society into a modern nation. He liked the term "model-building," preferring it to "theory" in his lectures. The distinction matters. A "model" is a social scientific theory, but it is not immutable, as the impression one sometimes gets from "theorists" regarding their works. I liked the choice of language. I also liked the optimism. Professor Siffin predicted that the nation's economic growth would lead to human rights and human dignity. He also emphasized the orchestrated efforts by the leadership and the general public toward the nation's developmental goal. Through fits and starts, Korea achieved this rough outcome. It was far from perfect. I often found myself in the role of critic of a repressive government. But his theory — his "model" — accurately described what happened in my homeland.

Finding the best paths to a citizens' welfare, economic development and education is the point of comparative administration. It does this by comparing and contrasting the experiences of many nations. Which nations best promote their citizens' well-being and how do they accomplish it? What are the vital elements of national development? Which government agencies are effective toward the end of development, and which ones aren't? Which countries' national infrastructure, health-care system, social services and vital public services are most effective and why? Why do others lag behind? These are the key questions. The transfer of institutions and technology from advanced nations to developing nations was hotly debated in Professor Siffin's class, as is the case today. So was the theory advanced by Samuel Huntington in the 1960s that political development is really about institutional development — that mobilization of political forces is not really what is first required — and about the stability of those institutions. Professor Siffin would later concentrate on institution-building in developing nations and spent time in Bangkok, Thailand and Manila, the Philippines.

* * * * *

My professor, who passed away several years ago, inspired the more than thirty-year teaching career I completed in 2006. I tried to imitate him throughout my teaching career, keeping in mind those words: "Life is zestful!"

Ever since, Christmas has reminded me of my teacher and his care for me, of both his encouragement of my academic work and my pursuit of happiness. Christmas means warmness at home, by the fireplace and at the dinner table with compassion and humanity. Christmas keeps warmth inside from the chill outside in December.

Several years after graduate school, my wife and I would name our son after him, and I would dedicate my first book humbly to him. I never had the chance to return his generous Christmas invitation. Every Christmas I continue to say, "Thank you, my great teacher, William J. Siffin." I miss you.

Life is zestful! I like to speak to the sparkling stars in the blue and dark sky of Christmas night. "Sparkling" is a more accurate word than "brilliant" when I think of my professor. This is the word his students and I would choose to describe him, because he was distinguished by his effervescent personality, in addition to scholarship.

Teachers in Korea are venerated in ways not so different from the reverence one retains for his parents or, in olden times, for the

Royal family. I keep the same reverence for Professor Siffin. Today, the reverential tradition lives on in Korea in the form of Teacher's Day, which occurs every May. I found many teachers at Indiana University worthy of veneration. Many teachers in the United States, I would later learn, are admirable. They evince that same quality I so admired and made me so grateful in Professor Siffin: Giving of themselves, above and beyond what is required.

CHAPTER 6

Environmental Administration

When I came to Indiana University in 1968, I had never heard of Environmental Administration. This was a new field, and it was also the name of a course in my graduate program. Indeed, the entire field of study — and environmentalism generally — was in its infancy. I visited the office of Professor Lynton K. Caldwell to find out more about the course he was offering. Caldwell was a tall, handsome man in his forties. We spoke about the course, then, there was a lull. He looked at me for a while, and asked me where I was from. When I answered that I was from Korea, he pulled the *New York Times* from his brief case, and urged me to read the front page article.

The front-page article reported that the Youngdungpo area in Seoul, Korea had the most polluted air in the world. I could not believe my eyes. I was shocked to learn that the Youngdungpo area could have such a dubious distinction. The worst air in the entire world! Before I left Korea, I read newspaper articles reporting that local anglers were catching strange-looking fish from the Han River. At that time, I did not think much about what might have caused these strange-looking Han River fish, except to conclude that perhaps these were caused by mutations, and that was it.

As Professor Caldwell explained, Environmental Administration is the study of air pollution, water pollution, and soil contamination. But more than this, it is about the study and the formulation of policies to prevent and to minimize these types of pollution. I regretted my ignorance, but he didn't hold it against me. Professor Caldwell instead opened my eyes to a new intellectual world. I appreciated his kindness.

* * * * *

I was lucky to be able to study under a man who, I soon learned, was the first political scientist in the United States and the world who

paid attention to environmental issues. He even contributed the first article on it, "Environment: A New Focus for Public Policy?" to *Public Administration Review*, the official journal of the American Society for Public Administration. That article was the first scholarly article to open the new world of the environment in public administration. He was seeing the dark side of the advancement of science and technology in modern society. In scientific and technological development, he saw hazards and risks to human life and to the ecosystem that were not readily apparent to most others in his field, or in society generally.

To learn more, I went to the University Library and checked out a couple of books authored by him. The insight there on the relationship between man and nature made sense to me. Professor Caldwell deplored the Christian ethic in which man dominated nature with science and technology, prompting in me for the first time serious thought about the limits of nature and the limits to which man could push the Earth.

In the classroom, Professor Caldwell lectured on the need for environmental impact statements to be undertaken for all government work. This eventually became an integral part of the 1969 National Environmental Policy Act. Later, when I worked for the U.S. Department of Defense, I learned the complexity and difficulty of actually conducting an environmental impact statement. The Act required environmental impact statements for all major public works projects, including but not limited to dam construction, shopping center development, and plant construction.

While studying environmental administration, I was able to rediscover things anew — in the poetry I loved and continued to read during this period in my spare hours. For instance, I re-read the 17th century Korean poet Yoon Sun-do's poems and discovered in them a kind of environmentalism. In his work, Yoon praises the water, rocks, pine trees, bamboo, and the moon. Perhaps one could best call him a naturalist, like John Muir. Yoon did not presage the seriousness of man's encroachment of nature, as Muir did in the 20th century, but he spoke with a reverence of the Earth that modern environmentalists could understand. I was enlightened when I read Muir's writing in environmental studies.

"Climb the mountains and get their good tidings. Nature's peace will flow into you as sunshine flows into trees," Muir wrote. "The winds will blow their own freshness into you, and the storms their energy, while cares will drop off like autumn leaves."

There was an obvious cross-cultural comparison to make here. Caldwell instructed me to compare Eastern culture versus Western cultures in their attitudes toward nature. I, a student from Korea, could see the traditional Korean cultural attitudes toward nature. The Koreans had for centuries tried to live with nature rather than harming nature. The land provided everything they needed. This way of living made sense for Korea as a poor nation, and indeed it played a role in keeping Korea poor.

When the South Korean government launched a series of five-year economic development plans in the 1960s, the new plans certainly were not based on this philosophy. Development meant science, technology, higher per capita income, promoting the wealth of the nation, the construction of dams and nuclear power plants, and a free market economy. New development plans already had spoiled parts of the Youngdungpo area, as the staggering news about the most polluted air confirmed.

Caldwell saw the Earth as a "spaceship Earth" — it was prescient. The study of environmental affairs is inherently international, he argued, for that reason. Because the object of environmental studies is the entire Earth — not the artificial boundaries of nation-states — those boundaries are meaningless for the purposes of environmental studies. The national approach, regional approaches, and the international approach toward the environment are, in this view, one in the same. Since I met my mentor, I have come to see "the world and I" — the environment as a single entity.

My first paper in this course covered Ibsen's "An Enemy of the People." In it, I argued that literary works such as Ibsen's could help the public more easily understand environmental affairs. Since the public is not expert on most matters of science and technology, it could come closer to a good understanding of these subjects through the more familiar medium of great literary works. Ibsen's play was a kind of cousin to environmental politics, I showed, and for that reason could be useful. Professor Caldwell regarded my paper highly, as having a new insight on environmental affairs.

Years later, I edited a special issue of *Environmental Management* devoted to the subject "Culture and the Environment." In that special issue, I tried to prove that environmental problems are rooted in each nation's culture. Every culture has its own character, its own weakness and its own strength, its beauties and its ugliness. A culture is any way of life, simple or complex. Understanding each nation's culture is the first step toward understanding each facet. Spaceship Earth, United Nations Conferences, and international management of environment and natural resources would each need to be understood in the context of the underlying national cultures.

Professor Caldwell was not only an inspiration but also a friend. He came to the Greyhound station in Bloomington to see me off to my first teaching job when I secured it at the University of Wisconsin-Whitewater in the summer of 1972. He gave me his new book, *International Environmental Policy*, as a farewell gift. The Greyhound Station in a small college town became the place of an unforgettable sending-off for this budding political scientist and environmentalist.

Even though Professor Caldwell died in August 2006, I still open the books that he signed and gave to me as gifts. I regularly return to his intellectual contributions as I think about this planet and ourselves, its inhabitants.

Later, as environmentalism blossomed, things grew complicated. The rise of NIMBYism — "not in my backyard" — impeded progress in some of the areas I worked on such as nuclear waste disposal. But then, there were problems on the other side of the spectrum. Idealism is a surprisingly difficult obstacle in conservation and environmental protection. At a time when realistic, pragmatic solutions were needed, far too many held out for unattainable goals. An undue idealism still prevails in much of academia and interest group politics today. When I had a chance to work inside the Pentagon in the 1980s, I realized that the real world could not accommodate all the idealism. At some point, we would need to compromise. The thousand pages of an Environmental Impact Statement (EIS) were later reduced to hundreds in the 1980s. Even thousands of pages could not cover all aspects of an EIS, anyway. We shrunk the workload because we became realistic.

Clean-up operation of the military installations' old chemical dumpsites cost millions of dollars. We could not invest that kind of money in the clean-up operation of Rocky Mountain arsenal in Colorado. So a "containment" policy was adopted. We always end up in compromise between the idealism and the reality. Money is always a limited resource. Limited knowledge and time are also part of limited resources.

Of course, all this was still a decade in the future.

CHAPTER 7

Working Hard

As was bound to happen, the money I had saved ran out in November. My friend, Kim P. Shee from Singapore, was working in the Village Pump as a cook. He arranged for a job for me washing dishes and assisting him. Shee, a doctoral student in the Political Science department, lent me the hand I needed. A minimum wage job would be just fine with me. I worked in the evening until midnight. It was an expensive bar and pizza house for students and the town people — no place I would be able to patronize regularly! But I got something out of the experience beyond the money that I wasn't expecting.

Working in the Village Pump turned out to be an excellent place to meet many students. I hadn't been expecting that. Some suggested to me to run for the foreign student senator's seat in the Indiana University Student Government during the spring semester. At that time, there was one seat available to represent 1,300 foreign students on campus. So I did. I entered and I won by a landslide over a student from a South American country. It helped a great deal that many students from Asia and the Arab regions voted for me — a great majority of the foreign students. And thus I became the first foreign student senator from the Asia-Pacific region. Most of the Asian students were not interested in student government or student politics and were basically studious. But I wanted to get more involved.

Student politics at Indiana University at that time resembled campus politics at many universities in the late 1960s. There were the town students who looked like Hippies, and then there were the Greek House students who looked like ladies and gentlemen. At the time I thought of it this way: One group was the common people and the other was the aristocrats. Now, this is very much an oversimplification, but there were reasons to at least think about it. One group was violently protesting the Vietnam War, and the other was mostly silent about it. One group was challenging and even rejecting basic American values, while the other was busily respecting them. Indiana University was an interesting place in the 1960s, as were all other universities in the United States, many roiling with social change and upheaval. I was fortunate to participate in student politics.

The Village Pump was a very good place to mingle in politics. Loud music, beer, pizza, dim light and young people all mixed well. The Vietnam War was always on the table. We had a mission to stop the war in Vietnam. Naturally, more immediate, school-oriented subjects like the coming tuition hike were also on the table. The town students vehemently protested the expected dramatic hike.

Even amid the tumult of the Vietnam War, I noted a mildness in American student politics that was absent in Korea. Student politics in Korea was extremely ideological. The far left was very strong, and the arguments were invariably pro-North Korea, anti-American and favoring unconditional reunification with North Korea. It was all about politics, and it was radical politics. These views were not part of the real world of national politics as it went on at the Blue House and the other arms of government in Seoul.

By contrast, what I saw on campus in the United States primarily concerned the elimination of social ills: Racial equality, ending the Vietnam War, protecting the environment and so forth. It was about policy. The student conversation was much less about existential national questions. Indeed, it was only a few shades left of the mainstream Washington political conversation. The same arguments one would hear in House and Senate and presidential campaigns about policy would crop up repeatedly in student debate. Student politics was part of the national political discussion in ways that was not the case in Korea. It was more issue-oriented. Politically activated students were, in short, "mainstream." Ideology was present but not overweening.

* * * * *

As a student senator, I considered it my duty to protest the tuition hike. But I was just a kitchen helper in the Village Pump. Mike King, vice-president of the student government, was a close friend of mine and editor of the underground newspaper at Indiana University. He could have run for president, but he yielded to a black student and instead ran for the office of vice-president in a sign of the racially progressive attitudes percolating in the university. Things were changing.

I found that, with some effort, I could sustain my destitute life with the minimum wages of a part-time job. I paid the Spring semester tuition with the money my parents gave to me when I left Korea. The money was so precious to me, and thus I could not spend it easily. This is how it went until, in the second year, I received a tuition scholarship. This meant I did not have to pay tuition, which was a large portion of my expenditures. I was much happier in the second year for that reason, once I was freed of a substantial financial burden.

* * * * *

During the three-month long summer vacation, I got a full-time job at the General Electric plant outside Bloomington. I commuted from my rooming house to the plant by bicycle. It was a quite long distance by bike, even if it was a country road. But I enjoyed riding the 15-mile distance in the morning and in the evening. My bicycling to the plant reminded me — a budding fan of American movies then, and especially latter on — of *Breaking Away*, starring Dennis Quaid. The movie was set in Bloomington. Here, there was an annual bicycle race that raised money for working students. Beloved in Bloomington, the race was immortalized on screen in this movie, and it came to mind often.

A foreign student coming to work by bike from the town, I soon began to make news as the new, unusual laborer at the plant. One fellow during the break in the assembly-line came to me: "Hey, where do you live in town?" "Third Street," I answered. He promised to give me a ride. It turned out that he lived just two blocks away. His name was Gary Capp. I will never forget his name — the first real, average American working guy I befriended.

Gary Capp was a kind neighbor to me. He was an ex-high school football player from Minnesota who loved playing the saxophone. One day he showed me one old newspaper scrap, which printed his touchdown story — the main glory of his previous life in his hometown.

I did not know why or when he settled in Bloomington. It was somewhat mysterious to me that he was living in a college town.

Of course, he was extremely popular among the ladies. Even though he was only high-school educated, he dated a college student majoring in arts and a graduate student majoring in English literature at the same time. He had some kind of a magic touch for the women. I did not know whether his saxophone, his good looks — he somewhat resembled Kevin Costner, the Hollywood actor — or his strong, built body attracted many women. These were just two of the women. He slept with them on different nights. I was pretty amazed to become a close friend of a real American playboy! He was nothing like any person I ever knew in Korea.

Now, he did not understand my life of working hard for only an advanced degree. He told me, "Life is short. You cannot sacrifice your youthful days, since they'll never come back." I listened to him. He invited me to a party at his rental house. My summer as a worker turned out to be much more fun than I expected, in part because of my new friend. He was a free spirit. His lifestyle was totally different from mine and the students I met in the classrooms and library. One time Gary invited me on a weekend hunting trip where I killed a mountain dove. Why did I kill such a peaceful bird? Well, I wasn't skilled enough to shoot any other animal, only the dove. So, in a kind of metaphor, I just followed him.

In the hot and humid summer nights, Gary invited me to go swimming in the quarry just outside the town. Summer in Bloomington was terribly hot. I could not sleep well some nights because I did not have an air conditioner. I had one small fan at the window of my room. For that reason I appreciated the invitation to cool off.

From time to time, the plant asked me to work overtime. Whenever I was asked, I was happy, because my overtime wage was one-and-a-half times the usual, sometimes double. I could not refuse those offers!

Gary didn't want to work overtime, but he did it anyway because of me. He wanted to give me a ride. I told him, "I can ride a bike!" But he picked me up in front of my house anyway on the way to the plant. I could not respond to him properly other than tears in my eyes.

Our friendship lasted many years after I left Bloomington. One day, my letter to him was returned to me. He moved out of that house without posting his new address. His free-spirited life ended in Bloomington. I shall never forget his saxophone and women, or women and saxophone. I don't know what happened to him.

* * * * *

Summer work on the assembly line took a serious toll on my body. Working overtime left an even heavier effect on my body. On the moving assembly line, I needed to be quick in performing the duties of my job. Coffee breaks were so precious to the assembly line workers. That was the break from the pressure. I earned a "sizeable" amount of money from the summer employment, and was able to send some of it to cover the cost of my sister's college tuition in Korea. The U.S. dollar was powerful at that time compared to Korean currency.

The assembly line produced quality refrigerators. The "Made in USA" tag attracted many people in the United States and throughout the world at that time. GE was the most powerful name among all manufacturers. I was part of that company. Rich Korean people could purchase GE refrigerators then and I had a hand in it. Some returning Korean students purchased the GE products and sent them to Korea by sea freight.

About ten years later, South Korea's LG began to produce even better refrigerators. My summer work in 1969 I can only consider a part of my Indiana life in the good old days! "Made in USA" has been challenged by Korea and many other developing nations. Resources are shared by many more nations, for example, China and India. One barrel of oil was $20 then and in 2008 it was unbelievably expensive, $140 or more. This, in its own way, was another lesson about the limited resources of the Earth. They are now so sought after by many more nations and people. The world was changing rapidly then, and it certainly is changing rapidly now.

Chapter 8

Landlady

Here's the story of an American original: My landlady. The woman who owned the one-story house on Third Street where I lived was an old, heavyset, conservative Christian woman in her 60s. She walked like a duck or, maybe, a boat undulating on the waves. Her natural habitat was a big living room with a couple of rocking chairs, one bedroom and a relatively big kitchen. The same floor had two small rooms that she rented out. I rented one room, and a student from India rented the other. The landlady used the front door that opened to Third Street, and we used the side door to an alley. So the landlady and we were separated. The basement was a kind of kitchen. It had a gas range, but no refrigerator. The gas range was useful for boiling water for coffee and instant ramen noodles.

The rent was $20 per week. I always paid my rent every four weeks in advance. It was the least expensive rent I knew of in Bloomington. My only regular contact with the landlady came when I paid the rent. Neither I nor my friend from India spent time in the room. We spent our time at the University. We just slept there, really. Once in a while, when she knew I was in my room, she knocked on my door and gave me a plate full of cookies she had baked. On other rare occasions she would invite me to her kitchen for coffee, where we chatted about the weather and the headline news from Bloomington.

Our relationship was amicable, to the point that, one Sunday, she asked me to go to her church. She knew that I was not religious. I joined her for a church service one Sunday. Her daughter gave us a ride to the church located outside of the town. We were all dressed up nicely. The church was not part of a major denomination. The church members were praying in a loud voice in an expressive way — this was new to me. Certainly, the church was not a quiet place to worship. She never asked me to go to her church after that one attendance.

So, it was amicable and peaceful — except for one occasion. I made the mistake of coming home intoxicated to the home of this very conservative Christian lady! She reacted in a way I'll never forget.

* * * * *

The night it happened, I stumbling home after a long bout of drinking. It was so bad that my Korean friend, Yong Moon Park, and a taxicab driver had to carry me to my room. Unfortunately for me, the landlady happened to see the scene. I was not aware of anything, much less her presence. On the following morning, I felt a cold air in the house. The winter-like cold air lasted a very long time. For a week, in fact, then, she called me into her quarter.

"Mr. Choi, you owe me an apology!"
"What apology?"
"You forgot the night you were dead."
"I don't remember—"
"Last Saturday night!"
"Oh, I heard from my friend what had happened later."
"Yes, you were dead. Mr. Choi, I saw you dead the night when your Korean friend brought you into your room. I was so frightened to see it."
I expected her Christian missionary speech.
"Mr. Choi, I did not drink even when my husband died, and my son died. How could you be in that noxious shape?"
I listened to her sincerely.
"It will not happen again, I promise you!"
"If I see you intoxicated again, I will kick you out of my house."

She was old-fashioned enough not to distinguish between her household — of which she evidently considered me a part — and the rights, such as they are, of a renter. They were not many in this case.

In our conversation, I learned one of the reasons she reacted so strongly. Her young son died from a car accident. He was a soldier hurrying back to the base after a party in town, and crashed. He was a victim of his own drunken driving. I was sympathetic to her over her son's story, and was trying to understand a mother's sorrow.

I did not have a car during my four years in Bloomington. I pedaled my bicycles. I lost four bicycles. Three of them were stolen at the University. One was stolen from Third Street. Who would steal a poor foreign student's bicycles? I was poorer than some American dogs and cats.

When I finished my work at Indiana University four years in, it was time to leave my stern landlady. She actually hosted a farewell party for me. Her two daughters and their family members came to her house with dishes, and we enjoyed one good dinner, our first and last, together. I presented a handbag and a shawl to her. She was happy to receive such gifts. She was happy when she announced to her family members that Mr. Choi received his doctorate degree as a resident of her house. I was happy, too.

She never understood why college students looked like beggars, or why I would come home "dead" one night. She did not forget to advise me: "Dr. Choi, you should dress up whenever you go to the classroom to lecture. She had complained that college students looked like beggars. I often responded to her: "Not all college students look like beggars. Some are always gentleman-like."

She never fully understood my friendship with Gary Capp, either. In her view, Gary was not a desirable fellow with whom I should be acquainted. She had her own bias and prejudice, as I did. That was the way she viewed things. Part of life is having bias and prejudice along with others' biases, isn't it?

But she was happy whenever I called her from Whitewater, Wisconsin in the following year, from my new job and new surroundings, just to say hello.

CHAPTER 9

The 1960s I Witnessed

The 1960s were a dynamic time. For most Americans, it began with the charismatic president John F. Kennedy and ended with the more common President Richard M. Nixon. In between those years, I lived through the rise and fall of some great people and the passing of some great events — Elvis Presley, the Beatles, Hippies, Jane Fonda, and anti-war demonstrations, for just a few that come to mind. Many of us who are old enough remember the 1960s with fondness yet nostalgia. This certainly describes my own reaction.

I was fortunate to have witnessed the last part of the 1960s in the United States, because I may never again see such passionate movements against the War and for environmental protection in my lifetime. That one tide has come and gone. Perhaps it will return in my lifetime.

The Vietnam War finally came to an end when anti-war demonstrators rallied behind the cause, crippling the administration in the public eye. Major television networks such as CBS, NBC and ABC reported the tragedy of the war on the morning, evening, and nightly news, in color. Jane Fonda was the Hollywood glamorization of the anti-war movement. Antiwar forces accepted Ho Chi Minh as a legitimate leader of all Vietnam. Fonda visited Hanoi. It was sensational. She praised Ho and the Viet Cong. I could not believe her speeches, because she could be seen as a traitor.

Meanwhile, I was writing in underground newspapers in Indiana. I was no apologist for American air power, that much was certain. I viewed the war as unjust, and I agreed that Ho Chi Minh, much as the West detested him, was the legitimate leader of that country. "Merciless American air attacks and bombing on the innocent Vietnam villages all for a French connection," I wrote. "Ho Chi Minh is the legitimate leader of all Vietnam from his long fight against the French imperialism."

Then the *Pentagon Papers*, the secret military reports revealing the U.S.'s involvement in the Vietnam War, were leaked to the New York Times and the Washington Post. That was amazing. The Supreme Court stood for the freedom of the press and allowed publication by the two major U.S. newspapers. Supreme Court justice William O. Douglas said, "What made the U.S. great is not the atomic bomb, but the First Amendment."

South Vietnam's leader Ngo Dinh Diem was a French-groomed and later U.S. backed leader who was ousted by a military coup d'etat and Vietnam's Buddhist monks. A supply of U.S. arms was famously stolen and smuggled into Viet Cong hands overnight. There were no suicide bombings like we see in Iraq and the Middle East today, but a U.S. military victory was impossibly hard to come by after the seven-year war. Finally President Lyndon B. Johnson yielded to the anti-war pressure groups. He blamed the defeat on Washington politics, not on the battlefield of Vietnam. He never recognized that the cause of defeat was rooted in the illegitimacy of U.S. actions in Vietnam. The U.S. soldiers were frustrated by their involvement in an un-winnable war, and the people at home were reflecting similar opposition to an unsupportable war. The expression of that frustration among service members was the My Lai massacre, in which U.S. soldiers slaughtered an entire village of innocent people.

The Vietnam War began when Ho Chi Minh defeated the French army in May 1954, after which the U.S. refused to accept the legitimacy of Ho as that nation's leader. The U.S. should have accepted Ho as the legitimate leader of Vietnam and it might have been able to negotiate a future with him, but it did not. The U.S. feared the spread of Communism in Southeast Asia and South Asia too greatly to consider that option. There are reasons to think these fears were overblown. Despite the predictions, the domino effect was not seen after Vietnam unified under Communist rule.

The French had created a puppet regime in South Vietnam under the twin guises of democracy and a market economy, even though this regime failed to deliver much of either. They supported this government anyway because Ho happened to be Communist. In 1957, Communists from both South and North Vietnam began attacking villages in South Vietnam. China, Russia and other communist countries sent aid to the Vietnamese Communists during the war. Non-communist countries supported South Vietnam. The U.S. became the chief ally of the South. It all seemed so inevitable — that, at least, was how it was regarded by the political elites of the 1950s and early 1960s.

In 1973, the U.S. agreed to a cease-fire, effectively accepting defeat in this seven-year war with the Viet Cong. South Vietnam could not withstand the Viet Cong and North Vietnamese attacks. The war was over in 1973. But the war had already been over when the U.S. Government yielded to the pressure mounting from the anti-war popular sentiment in the United States. President Johnson lost support even though he had achieved success in many of his proposed Great Society programs. He was challenged by Senator Eugene McCarthy, an unknown but strongly anti-war senator from Minnesota in the Democratic primaries.

The predicted domino effect, that is, that many more countries would become Communist countries if we were to abandon Vietnam to its fate, never happened. In time, Vietnam became a market-economy, closer to the United States politically and economically than to a totalitarian state. In time, the Soviet regime disappeared and East European nations were liberated in the 1990s. So, the end of ideology was predicted as early as the 1960s, and it was actualized in the 1990s.

During those years as a college student, I contributed a lengthy article against the war to an underground newspaper in which I pointed out that peasant nationalism against Western imperialism, more than the force of international communism, was the major political mover in Vietnam and China. I joined the anti-war demonstrations as the foreign student senator representing all foreign students in the Indiana University Student Senate and made a speech in front of the students condemning the war. I was admonished by the Office of Foreign Students at Indiana University not to join such a radical movement sponsored by the town students, the so-called Hippies. These undesirable, pot-smoking hooligans earned the ire of university administrators. Possession of marijuana was illegal. Young people, of course, experimented anyway, out of fun or curiosity.

I was proud of my activities in the student movement. However, toward the end of the 1960s, the underground newspaper published by Mike King, vice-president of the IU Student Government, and his friends, lost its popularity and support. Its demise was predictable, because the students were seeing the demise of the Vietnam War and one revolutionary era. The new wave was heading to shore. The pendulum of history was moving from the left to the right. The system was reestablishing homeostasis.

* * * * *

The Beatles were popular in the 1960s. During the middle and late 1960s, they helped to give rock music a new direction. Most earlier rock music had been based primarily on a strong beat, but the Beatles' music contained a new sense of melody. Their chord progressions were also more complex, and the lyrics of their songs were more imaginative and meaningful than the bands that preceded them. John Lennon and Paul McCartney composed several songs of social criticism and anti-war sentiment that struck a chord in me and in others, including "Nowhere Man" (1965) and "Eleanor Rigby" (1966). They also wrote such beautiful ballads as "Michelle" (1965) and "Yesterday" (1965). After I arrived in the US came "Hey, Jude" (1968), "Come together" (1969), and "Something" (1969). The group broke up in 1970 after drifting apart in the late 1960s, like many things of that period — after the 1960s, they began to lose their urgent purpose. The artists went on to do their own things. People wanted a new music, just as they looked for a new fashion in the spring.

Born alongside the anti-war movement was the environmental movement in the United States. The Earth photographed from the moon by the Apollo astronaut was beautiful, with blue oceans and white clouds. This was a watershed moment. The Earth suddenly took on a personality, like that of an entity imbued with a delicate life. A war on this beautiful Earth was not acceptable at all. That earth photo created a new awakening.

* * * * *

50

Suddenly, activists became aware of the polluted air and polluted water in the industrial areas and Great Lakes. The Santa Barbara oil spill shocked the country when it covered the seagulls with black oil, and caused the death of many living things in the coastal areas. Dead black seagulls were on the cover of Newsweek magazine after the war had occupied that same spot for many weeks. The Cuyahoga River was so polluted that it caught on fire. The general public finally became aware of the dangers, including cancer, represented by the "chemical society."

Earth Day became a reminder to young people: Conserve energy and natural resources, and protect the Earth. The National Environmental Policy Act of 1969 was a key moment. On the morning of January 1, 1970, President Nixon signed the Act.

During this period, a strain of thought emerged inside environmentalism and the antiwar movement that, in my view, had little to do with either. It was amazing to see the darkness many people saw in American values, political and economic systems, and advanced science and technology. I did not share that same outlook. I shared a serious concern with the environment, and opposition to the war. I recognized the dark side of greedy Western capitalism, which was sometimes at war with nature. But I felt that I was witnessing an anti-American movement within the environmental movement that was unrelated to the core purposes. I was happy with the thrust of environmentalism generally. The value of Nature was being discovered or rediscovered by a great many people, which could only be a good thing. I just didn't see much of value in the peripheral phenomenon.

In retrospect, I do think that the beginning of the conversation about the environment as it emerged in the 1960s should have brought about a more influential conservation about the environment. It should have wrenched better policies out of the United States. For a variety of reasons, progress has not taken place the way I thought it would. I figured that a wealthy, moneyed society like the United States could afford sound environmental policies like no other nation. Of course it would adopt them! The United States would lead the way. But it turns out that the foundations of a market economy and capitalistic society are very solid and difficult to change. America's elected leaders resisted the sorts of tough environmental policies that most experts in the field today agree are necessary. To this day I still admire the Scandinavian model of a more socialistic government and strong environmental protection. I was wrong to conclude that a wealthy nation would automatically move along the same path. It certainly made sense to me then, and it continues to make sense to me today. But not, evidently, to the majority of Americans.

The 1960s were also a period of welcome heightened scrutiny and awareness of racial discrimination and sexual bias, exposed to the naked eyes of young American people, in reality for the first time. It was a time of new ideas about the divinity of nature in young American people who were examining values in Confucianism and Buddhism. Lao Tzu was emerging as an important centerpiece for study in the humanities and the social sciences. It was a time of incredible tumult.

* * * * *

Now, looking back from the vantage point of the present, I know I'm not the only one who sees parallels in the 2008 presidential election. Barack Obama is a new phenomenon who is resurrecting the 1960s. I can see a kind of reincarnation, a revitalization of the ideas of the 1960s. Mr. Barack Obama is the newly elected president of the United States in 2008. A black man with a funny name, funnier than my name, is elected to the highest office of the United States and the world. Unbelievable! That is fantastic! This is my reaction as a Korean-American.

It has been a long journey of progress toward equality and human rights from the 1960s to 2008. Mr. Barack Obama's victory is historical and revolutionary. It could be the start of the second wave of American political and economic history. That is certainly one great sign of the progress in American history.

CHAPTER 10

Poetry and Art

Poetry has always held a special place for me, beginning in my youth in Korea. I loved to read poetry, write poetry, talk about it, read it aloud, meet its authors and live the life of a person who appreciates poetry deeply. From an early age, my parents knew this. I loved literature of all kinds, but I loved poetry more. They hoped I would grow up to be a Pulitzer Prize-winning poet or a Nobelist! I never quite accomplished those feats. I did, however, make poetry an indispensable part of my life as I experienced it and reflected upon it.

I have an especial fondness for poems about nature: the four seasons, the ocean waves and more. I also have a fondness for poetry about love, and for reflections on the nature of poetry itself – a common enough poetic theme.

Over the years, my poetry has found its way into journals near and far, in the United States, Korea and elsewhere, of which my parents could be proud. It appeared in high-school newspapers and literary magazines to college newspapers and even the most prestigious literary magazines in Korea. Later, I began translating my poems from Korean into English to publish them in the *Korea Times* and *Korea Herald*, two major English-language daily newspapers in Seoul. During my time in the Philippines I published in the *Manila Chronicle Magazine's* front and back covers. Just like a mountaineer seeks to conquer the highest mountain, I always find a media outlet to publish my poetry wherever I have been. My life has been poetry and poetry has been my life to some very strong degree. I have been honored on many occasions. That being one of my father's wishes, I think he would be happy to know it.

After I passed the comprehensive exam before writing a doctoral dissertation, I felt an emptiness, a void in my life. I had a desire to fill that void. I wrote very long letters to my parents and teachers in Seoul, but the letters could not fill the void. Then, I thought of starting a poetry-art ensemble. It would make sense to do it in the Indiana University Memorial Union Building, which could house it well. That was my dream. I wrote 20 poems during my time in Indiana. I wanted to present my poems with illustrating artwork. Finishing my dissertation was less urgent for me. I assembled five fine art students on campus who could do the work, and let them select their favorite poems. Komelia Hong Ja Okim, Susan E. Hinkle, Karen Elshout, Janet Smith, and Carol Wamsley were the five. One high school literature book inspired me to find a photographer to illustrate my poems. I found David Mather outside the University. He was a young photographer at the Daily Herald-Telephone, a town newspaper.

Then, I managed to win financial support from the Indiana University Student Government for my proposed show. I needed a small amount of money to provide the materials for the art students and the photographer. Mike King, the Vice President of the Student Government, was very receptive to my idea. I had published some of my poems in his underground newspaper and he knew my work. He asked me to write a statement to open the poetry-art ensemble. I composed the following statement and handed it to him:

"The poetry-art ensemble is popular among Korean poets and artists. I know this is also popular in the rest of East Asia. I have not yet seen this kind of poetic expression in this country. Therefore, my ensemble is one way of introducing an aspect of Asian culture."

"This exhibition is a poetic review of my two years at Bloomington. My poems are a source of comfort to me in my native land and in the United States. I have published twenty poems in the Indiana Daily Students and literary magazines. I wish and hope that my fellow students, professors and neighbors will see my life in the form of poetry. I was a poet before I became a graduate student of political science. I am proud of my poetry. I came from a country in which the poets are considered stars in the blue and dark night sky."

"As a foreign student senator, I have a desire to contribute something to this University community I love very much. Many foreign students do not see their precious life under the pressure of academic works. This show is my expression of gratitude to my University."

My Sail

A gull
And solitude with the solidity of a thing.
My sail shines fresh venturing alone
In the shadow of the Pacific.
What am I searching for in a distant land?
What have I cast off in my native land?
The waves are playing, the winds whistle,
And the mast bows and creaks.
Alas! I am searching for happiness!
Below the soul a stream of glistening azure,
Between the vast expanse of the sky
And the waters.

To the Flowers of Indiana

Running away from the university and America
I become a little animal in the woods.
Flowers picked are arranged into a meaning
And then presented to a girl on the way to town.

The girl, now a lady of my dreams and my ideals,
Would she be in the woods
As a little creature as I was in Indiana?
Would she relay a meaning to the next generation?

Ten years thereafter another bouquet;
Would this young man be passing it
To another girl on a hillside path?
Life waves in vain, but knows no bounds.

Would there be a stranger?
Would he hand down flowers to the next generation?
The sun is glistening at the foot of a hill
After a shower, when twilight is in the field.
Leaning against the sunset,
A poet exhausts his view.

Self-Portrait

Look, a youth beside the river
Who is playing with words.
He has sensitive fingers
Like a fisherman.
When his fingers touch the words,
Meanings come out to the world
From a hard metaphor box.

He is an amateur burglar
Who breaks the black box,
A sunken treasury.

He returns to the old age
As if the water carried old meaning
To the sea
And new meaning from the mountain stream.

No one knows he is an amateur, sometimes
Professional burglar.
Everyone in town knows he is a fisherman.

America

Rome of the twentieth century,
This Rome shall not collapse
Like the other.

The USA is translated as the "Beautiful Country"
In Chinese characters,
That translation is accurate.
The country's nature is beautiful.

The millionaires and the poor enjoy
The same hamburger and coca-cola.
That is equality and democracy,
The poor deny any social divisions in the USA.

The more he is paid,
That much harder he works for a while.
Capitalism kills poetry,
But there are many fine poets in the USA.

After eight hours' work,
A few drinks of beer,
Sleeping is fairly sound and peaceful.

From Alaska to Florida,
Deserts are dancing on the hot tin roof,
And lakes are placid under the moonlight.
We don't need a world trip in
A continent between the Pacific and
The Atlantic.

Everyone keeps a connection with the home country,
And everyone wants to go home, but cannot.
Why? Why not?
Can we find the answers in cold drinks?
Sleeping in rugged individualism
Is the most attractive in the USA.

* * * * *

Mr. King told me that he was shocked to know that my poem, "Nostalgia," had been dedicated to Wendy Franley, a beautiful student from Northern Indiana. Wendy happened to be his high school classmate. He stated that not many men could approach her, because she was one of the most attractive women. We laughed. I told him, a student in English, "Poetry can attract a beautiful woman!"

"Yearn, where did you meet Wendy?"
"At the swimming pool."
He was surprised to know my first meeting with her at a swimming pool.
"Mike, I am proud of my being a poet."
"You better."
He was my favorite friend at Indiana University.

He worked out a small amount of money for my show. I was happy to provide the painting and photographer's materials to the art students and the photographer. I spent some time with them during their production of good art works. I went out to accompany David Mather for his shooting. He produced a good work from the dark room to juxtapose my poems in his photography. I spent some time in his dark room, too. I showed one American high school literature book containing poems of Robert Frost, Carl Sandburg, and John Mansfield with illustrating photography. At the end, we were satisfied with our work.

The show opened in October 1970 in the North Lounge of the Union Building for one month. The Indiana Daily Students and the Daily Herald-Telephone covered my poetry-art ensemble two or three times nicely. The Indiana University Public Information Office disseminated a foreign student's poetry with artwork to many outside media. The Associated Press and United Press International even picked up my story. My father in Seoul knew of my show in Bloomington. However, my first name was wrongly translated into Korean from English: Yang from Yearn. But the picture was mine. My father who loved and respected poetry was so happy when he read an article about his son's poetry-art ensemble in the United States. He framed the article in his living room for all his life.

I invited all my teachers to the show. Professor Alfred Diamant sent me a note: "Yearn, your poetry is better than your prose." He was critical of my English, and edited a couple of pages in every research paper I submitted to him. I accepted his comment as a compliment! He could still remember my disobedience to my faculty adviser's advice to take an English course.

After the show, the art students got back their paintings, except for one by Susan Hinkle, "Self-Portrait." It was my own self-portrait. All of my photographer's works were presented to my teachers and to Dwight Waldo at Syracuse University, whom I admired, and Indiana University Chancellor Herman B. Wells, former president of the University and a great educator. I appreciated David Mather's generous donation of his works for my gifts.

* * * * *

The Union Building is still my favorite spot at Indiana University. I used to read and study in a spacious room furnished with comfortable chairs and couches, while sitting by the fireplace during the winter months, in a spacious room in the Union Building. The North Lounge is my special place because my most unforgettable exhibit was on its four walls in the fall of 1970. Though I was a poor foreign student, I considered myself rich — as a foreign student, I owned all of Indiana University in an important sense. Years later, Hanryu (a poetry-art ensemble) is a new word popular in Japan, Southeast Asian nations, and in the United States. Korean films and, arts are well accepted by foreign nations. My poetry-art ensemble made its contribution to the rise of Hanryu in the 1970s at Bloomington, Indiana. Yes, I was rich.

CHAPTER 11

My First Teaching Job in Wisconsin, and Marriage

The United States is, has been, and hopefully always will be an open society. This point means something to new arrivals that it may not for native-born Americans. The latter do not need to think much about visas, work permits, immigration status, freedom to work, personal freedom and the like. But when I finished my Ph.D, I wasn't ushered out of the country. Just as I had been able to work to pay my way through school, now this foreign student would have a chance to seek a college teaching job once I completed my dissertation. I was free to speak, teach, research and write as I and my colleagues saw fit, and I would now be free to compete for a permanent job. What made the United States great, I thought then and still think today, is this openness.

At that time, the job market was tight. Ph.D. overproduction was the norm at that point since so there were so many students who pursued a degree to avoid the draft. So my chances were not very good. My teachers did not encourage nor discourage me. Some members of the Indiana University faculty thought that I could return to Korea to teach Korean students. But I was not comfortable returning to my home country. It was still ruled by Park Chung-hee, the military general-turned-to-president, and I did not want to have to teach under the repressive conditions typical of the Park years. A person could not speak freely back then — indeed things didn't improve appreciably in Korea in this regard until the 1990s. I also wanted to enjoy the fruits of a teaching career in the United States. Then there was the fact that teaching here would not harm my prospects of returning to Korea to teach; it would probably help it.

So, I drove with a handful of classmates one April morning in 1972 to the American Society for Public Administration conference in New York City, prospecting for jobs. All day we drove, and in the evening, we settled in the Washington, D.C. area for one night. I met my old friend from Yonsei University, Mr. Hyoung-Yul Kim, who was studying at the University of Maryland, College Park.

Once in New York we attended the panel discussions, met a couple of potential employers at the conference and networked. That was my first trip to New York City — unforgettable. After one week at the ASPA conference, I found the Association of Asian Studies conference was scheduled in New York City. So I stayed one more week, as a tourist. I saw Central Park, Macy's Department Store, Tiffany's, Lincoln Center, Radio City, the Broadway, the Rockefeller Center, the Modern Arts Museum, the Guggenheim Museum, the New York Metropolitan Museum, Chinatown, the Empire State Building, the Statue of Liberty, the *New York Times*, and the *Wall Street Journal*, among others. I was amazed by the sky-high cityscape darkened in the night under the full moon on the left corner. I was standing on the New Jersey side of the Hudson River.

In May, there was a Midwestern American Political Science Association conference in Chicago, where I landed a job interview with the chairman of the Political Science Department of the University of Wisconsin-Whitewater. It was a one-year appointment. The incumbent was on leave and I would fill the one-year vacancy. He was interested in me, and I was relieved to have a possible offer. I did not have much of a choice.

When I returned to Bloomington, he called me for my visit. He invited me as one of the three candidates for the open position. I went to his campus, and delivered a lecture in the classroom on American Government, and was interviewed by the existing faculty members and by the vice president of the university. It went smoothly until the interview in the office of the vice president. He asked me whether I could teach an American Government course, which was a bread-and-butter course for all undergraduate students. He was questioning my four short years in the United States. His question was legitimate. I had to defend myself. I responded, "Four years has been long enough for me to know American society and American Government! Forty years may not be enough to know American Government to some people. But to me, four years are good enough."

I smiled, and asked a question: "Sir, do you know Alexis de Tocqueville who wrote the classic *Democracy in America* after he traveled to America a century ago?" I then proceeded to explain what Tocqueville (1805-59), the great French political thinker, meant to me as a student of the United States and a native of Korea. Tocqueville was a passionate champion of freedom — society's freedom from state control, and the citizen's freedom from government interference. In the early 1830s, Tocqueville traveled to America, discovering there a stable and peaceful democracy unlike anything that he had seen in France. French politics was turbulent after the downfall of Louis XVI. I read *Democracy in America* in admiration. Korean politics in the 1960s was turbulent as well, lacking in the elements Tocqueville identified — and here I was, with a unique perspective to appreciate it today. I thought I made a good pitch, illustrating my knowledge of American political principles and putting it in the context of my personal experience as a Korean.

He was still suspicious of my coming to Whitewater. I did not receive the letter of contract from the University of Wisconsin-Whitewater in a week or so. I thought I had been denied by the vice president. It was awful. But, to my great relief, a couple of weeks later, I received the contract. What a joy!

After I landed in Whitewater, I found out that the students and the faculty supported me against the vice president's will. I got the teaching job, and I was happy. God helps those who help themselves. I thanked the Lord, and my parents' prayers and I sent my letters to my teachers in Korea.

At this point I should say a thing or two about my religious background, since, as I just mentioned, I prayed in thanks to God when my job came through. I am a Christian, but I was not always "as Christian" as I am today, and through my family I am also heir to a long Confucian tradition. My first regular exposure to Christianity came at Yonsei University where I was an undergraduate and graduate student. Yonsei is a Christian school founded by American missionaries more than 100 years ago. It was there that I began to read the Bible regularly. It was part of my coursework. At the time I read the Bible as a literary work, not as a religious text, as I was not a religious or church-going person at the time.

My parents prayed for their son's good health and safety, but they prayed to our ancestors, not to God per se. Ancestor worship is part of the Confucian ethic, and our family was steeped in it. During my college days, though, I began attending church near the university sporadically and later, as a graduate student, went to my landlady's church. Over time, being in America, I became a Christian man who believes in Christ. Being here, and seeing the import of Christianity in American life, opened the door for me as I gravitated to Christian belief.

*****

Elated to have a job, at long last, it was at this point that my parents began in earnest attempting to find my bride. They waited what for them was a very long time — until I got a teaching job. This was only a one-year job, I cautioned them. But they did not care much. At this point they thought I was on a continuously successful mission impossible in the United States! I could do no wrong.

As even these few sentences suggest, marriage and courtship at the time in Korean families were handled very, very differently than they are in the United States and also in Korea today. Marriage was a matter of utmost family import. It was viewed much less as a personal choice the way it is in contemporary society and instead as a reflection of the values and standing of one's family. Thus did my parents — and the parents of my soon-to-be bride — pair us before we ever met. We began exchanging letters. I sometimes wonder whether my wife and I were the last of our generation to make a "picture bride" of her! And a "picture groom" of myself. But my bride and I would accept our parental arrangements and over the years we built a strong love. Difficult as it may be for modern Westerners to imagine being in this position, we regarded it as normal at the time, and our marriage moved from a pairing of unfamiliar young adults to loving partners for life.

*****

The first semester is always the hardest for new teachers. I prepared for many hours as I readied myself to teach 9 hours worth of college courses, 3 of them. My preparation was always too little because

I found trouble filling up nine hours. So I urged my students to ask questions and solicited their comments on my lecture at the end of each class. They were usually quiet or silent. Once in a while, several students asked me questions. They were rescuing me in the last five minutes. I liked the Q & A. If I had time still, I discussed the current issues in the American Government and society. I did not like giving one-sided lectures at all. I also realized my knowledge on American Government was very limited — a fair question this was from the vice president — so, not wanting to prove that his worries would turn into a problem, I spent all my weekends preparing for my lectures.

The year 1972 was a year for new federal-state-local fiscal relationships, and Federal Revenue Sharing, a new "federalist" idea proposed by President Richard M. Nixon, was under much discussion. So I conducted a survey in the State of Wisconsin and Wisconsin local governments: How were governments planning to spend federal revenue sharing money? Research was always a fun part of my teaching job. My results, published in an academic journal of local governments, got some attention and helped convince my critics in the university that I was fully engaged in American politics.

It also happened that 1972 was the year of the Stockholm United Nations Conference on the Human Environment. My teacher, Lynton K. Caldwell, was one of the main architects of the international environmental conference. At the Stockholm conference, Nairobi, Kenya was designated for the headquarters of the UN Environmental Programme. It soon became an environmental symbol of Third World power against the United States and European power. Now, from the beginning, politics between the rich and the poor nations had dominated international discussions of environmental affairs. I have been watching the international environmental politics ever since with some disappointment, hoping for a more rational, problem-solving approach.

* * * * *

My soon-to-be wife and I had been exchanging letters for several months. This was in preparation for our traditional Korean arranged marriage, in this case arranged from overseas. Bong Hee Kim — that was my wife's maiden name — came to her uncle's house in Maryland during the Christmas holidays. Our two families in Korea arranged the wedding at her uncle's home in Rockville. At the wedding at Rockville, I met my bride for the first time. "Bong" means a large bird. As it happens, the "Hong" of my own name also means a big bird. The two are compatible, we immediately thought! We were married, both in our mid-twenties with our lives ahead of us.

We spent our honeymoon traveling by bus: From Washington to Bloomington, and then to Whitewater, Wisconsin. By Greyhound Bus! In Bloomington, we stayed at my fond old Union Building, where my poetry-arts ensemble was held. I showed my beloved school, campus, and introduced my teachers to her.

In one important respect my bride could not enjoy the honeymoon period at all: The Spring semester of 1973 was also a time for job searching. I was preparing for my departure to another unknown place, while also preparing three courses. My situation contributed to a painful adjustment to her new life in the United States. I still feel guilty for burdening her with my unstable, challenging early years.

During the honeymoon, her comforts came from a couple of Korean-American faculty members, Ralph Song and Kirk Kim, who were kind to her. So were their families. We purchased our car, a 1972 Chrysler Satellite, with $3500, and visited a Wisconsin dairy farm and apple orchard, Lake Geneva, the Milwaukee Brewers' Stadium in the famous American beer town, and Madison, home of the University of Wisconsin; plus one long weekend trip to Minneapolis-St. Paul, Minnesota to see our old friends, Mr. and Mrs. Ki-Suk Lee, my elementary school friend, who was studying urban geography at the University of Minnesota in that Spring semester. In one small class of 25, we earned our doctorate degrees from two decent American universities. Our friendship is still alive, and lasting forever.

Thankfully, I soon had a job offer from Old Dominion University in Norfolk, Virginia. We drove a long distance from Whitewater to Norfolk in the end of August of 1973. Our passage was: Wisconsin to Illinois, Indiana, Ohio, West Virginia, and Virginia. Crossing the mountains and hills in West Virginia in the summer time was memorable to both of us. It could have been our second honeymoon on the road. We saw the destitute mining towns in West Virginia from the winding roadside — before beginning our new life in Virginia.

CHAPTER 12

Norfolk, Entrance and Exit

And so we headed off to Norfolk, the second medium-size town in which I settled after Seattle. Norfolk is a maritime hub on the Virginia shores a few hours' drive from Washington, D.C.; Bloomington and Whitewater, the two college towns in Indiana and Wisconsin where I taught, are quite different. Norfolk during the spring was beautiful: azaleas, magnolias and dogwood flowers against the background of blue ocean waters. It gets warmer much earlier; it stays that way longer.

At the time of my arrival, E. Grant Meade, a soft-speaking gentleman, diplomat and military officer, was the chairman of the Political Science Department of Old Dominion University. He came to the Norfolk airport to pick me up for my job interview. He drove me to a downtown hotel through the residential areas scenic with flowering trees and gardens. The ocean made the area more scenic. Sometimes the water would come into someone's front yard from his or her neighbor's back yard in the residential areas.

As I would later learn, Meade served the United States Military Government in Korea in 1945-1948 as a military officer. He still kept his young officer's memories from Korea. He led and guided me through the town, a middle-class place and very clearly a Navy town. He told me that people were nice, but not as sophisticated as the Midwesterners. We didn't speak much about Southern bias and prejudice, about which I would later learn a thing or two.

I met the departmental members, and toured the town. Three members were foreigners: one Canadian retired general teaching international politics, one Iranian fellow on leave, and one Indian teaching legislative behavior. Meade recruited them. He was the first and founding chairman of the Political Science department. I visited the Meade residence near the edge of the waters. I bantered that the department was a small-scale version of the United Nations when I joined. All were nice. In the following week, I was offered a teaching job.

I like the word: "Tidewater." The Tidewater area covers the cities of Norfolk, Portsmouth, Virginia Beach, and Chesapeake. Norfolk and Portsmouth were old towns, and Virginia Beach and Chesapeake were new emerging towns. I could see the balancing forces of the old and new towns, one set standing rather complacent, the other building itself aggressively.

Then there was the Atlantic Ocean. Here was the most attractive natural asset of them all in the Tidewater area. The dynamics of vast blue water and seagulls are always an affectionate thing to poets and writers. As they were for me.

I settled at the Larchmont apartments, a modest place within walking distance of the university. A one-bed, furnished room was enough for my wife and me. My colleague, John Ramsey, found this apartment upon my request. He was a kind person. I still think he is a very decent man. He happened to be the chairman when I faced my tenure evaluation five years later, a story that did not end well — more on that later. Our relationship in the end was not good.

By a three-to-two vote, I could not obtain the tenure from the university. This made my departure from the university my first failure in the United States. It was a sad time. It happened entirely against my will.

In between my entrance and exit, I became the father of our two children: Our son Jay was born in August 1976 and our daughter Joyce was born in February 1978. I felt sorry for my wife and my children following my failure at work.

But, for all the good that happened there, especially my children's birth, Norfolk is a town I will never forget. My poems were translated and published in Portuguese in Brazil. A professor and his graduate students in comparative administration at the University of Espirito Santo helped me do it. My Op-Ed pieces were published in the *Virginian-Pilot*. I owned a house in Virginia Beach for the first time in my life. But I had to leave the town against my will. It was sad.

Though my first five years at the university were evaluated as good, I failed to get tenure at the end of five years. What an irony! Well, irony is a part of life.

Life is relatively simple for college professors. Even though the campus has changed greatly over the decades, their lives still are relatively simple. Teaching, research and professional service are the three criteria that formulate the basis for evaluations just about everywhere from Harvard to any small college. Old Dominion University also set up such criteria for their faculty evaluations.

Teaching:

Teaching can constitute 50 percent or more of the total evaluation. Based on the weight of the teaching criterion, research and professional services would make up their respective portion for the remainder of the evaluation. Teaching is naturally (or should be) the most important thing for faculty evaluations. College professors are basically teachers. An evaluation of teaching is based upon the syllabus prepared and the student evaluations of the teacher and course at the end of each semester. I received high marks on student evaluations during my teaching career. I tried to improve my teaching ability all the time. For example, I attended the American Political Science Association-sponsored seminars designed to improve the teaching of public policy courses at Georgetown University one summer, and at the University of Missouri another summer.

Research:

College professors should be engaged in research activities and produce their research results and outcomes as research papers, books, or patents. Social scientific research works are published in academic and scholarly journals. Ideally, we create new knowledge and information to improve social institutions and democratic systems that eventually advance the quality of human life. Research activities will enhance teaching, too. I constantly conducted research projects and published my research papers. I also presented them at the American Society for Public Administration conferences. I was selected as a National Aeronautics and Space Administration summer faculty fellow for forecasting civic aviation in the United States, and produced a group report, *Avionics: Projections for Civil Aviation 1995-2000.*

Professional Service:

College professors are also members of professional organizations. They are supposed to be active in their respective organizations. All organizations have their annual meetings. Some serve as presiders and some as paper presenters. Some just attend the meetings to meet their old friends. I did my part by serving the American Society for Public Administration's Southeast regional organization as a member of its executive board and I presented papers at the ASPA's national and regional meetings.

Community Service:

Professional service is not necessarily the same as community service. Some college and university faculty evaluations include community service. Community service is a faculty member's service to the community in which he or she lives and where the university is located. I conducted a series of public forums sponsored by Virginia Foundation for the Humanities and Public Service inviting mayors, councilmen and women, bureaucrats and citizens to the forums on local governments, bureaucracy and democracy, and published the proceedings. I also contributed to the *Virginian-Pilot*'s Op-Ed page, and to the *Donga Ilbo*, a Korean language daily newspaper based in Washington, D.C. as a columnist. My columns appeared twice a week during my stay at Old Dominion University. I served the Tidewater Korean-American community as its elected president. I organized a concert at Chrysler Hall that brought Koreans and Americans closer via music. I chose Anton Dvorak's America as the opening music to be played by Korean and American musicians, singers, pianists, violinists and cellists in the Tidewater area.

Every year, I went to the Office of the President to make my case for a higher pay raise over my colleagues. I always received higher pay, because I did more than my colleagues in all of the criteria.

In the tenure evaluation, all my achievements were flatly denied:

Teaching:

My evaluators said I was only popular among the students because I did not offer much homework. More than this, they said that I could not possibly be a good teacher because I have a heavy Korean accent. I knew a few students complained about my accent, and my liberal political views on American politics. I could not defend my accent, but I said to my students: Henry Kissinger has his accent, yet who complained about his?

Research:

My published works were supposedly not good enough. Well, the great majority of the departmental members did not produce a single publication during their career. How could they judge my publications in scholarly refereed journals? I had published my works in such journals as *Public Personnel Management, State Government, Bureaucrat, Planning and Administration, World Affairs,* and the *Illinois Quarterly,* among others. I also published articles in the *Public Administration Times,* and the *American Political Science Association News,* the two professional organizations' newspapers to which I belonged. The person who received tenure just before me had published his single article in the *Virginia Social Science Journal.*

My publications could not compete with those of the Harvard faculty. However, I believed that my works deserved the tenure at Old Dominion University. The department chairman questioned a paper I had coauthored with my graduate student, Ellen Posivach, who was a high school teacher. I gave one of my papers on literature and bureaucracy, and invited her to have co-authorship of the paper because she had her undergraduate education in English literature. My colleagues thought she was the primary author and I was the secondary author, or I was using her paper as my own. They were terribly wrong. She thanked me for my invitation. She wrote a letter about the situation to the college and university review boards, but it did not change the department's decision.

Professional Service:

They made no comment!

Community Service:

Here, again, they made no comment!

I appealed to the college and university review boards. I could not win. The review board said that the university's expectations for junior faculty members were higher. However, it was hard for me to measure the degree of difference in the expectations placed upon junior faculty as opposed to senior faculty. I went to the Equal Employment Opportunity Commission in Washington, D.C. to register my complaint against Old Dominion University based on racial and ethnic bias and prejudice grounds; however, my complaint was mounted by a tremendous backlog. The EEOC lawyer did not give me hope. I was helpless. There were so many civil rights organizations in the United States, but they were useless to me. There may be so many people who are helpless in this world at this moment. They lament the fact that justice may not always prevail in this world.

So I began preparing my departure.

Faculty for Justice, a small group, was organized to protest the university's decision against my tenure. But under pressure from the university, efforts by this group were futile and lost its vitality in a month or two. The university had a lawyer. When the Faculty for Justice was exposed to the newspapers, I received midnight calls threatening my life. I still remember a harsh voice from the other end of the telephone line: "You are not even a nigger. Why do you complain in this country? Go home! I will kill you!" My wife feared such calls, and suggested that we move out of town.

My Indian colleague confessed to me at the end of the turbulence: "Yearn, I am sorry. I voted against you in the tenure decision, because there were too many foreigners in the Department. If I voted for you, you would have won the tenure by a three-to-two vote."

His confession still puzzles me: Who was the other person who voted for my tenure? E. Grant Meade plus one more. I still do not know the one person among the five tenured faculty members in the department at Old Dominion University, who silently and anonymously supported me. Of course, Meade did not disclose his vote for me. I just counted on his vote for me.

I decided to leave Old Dominion University, even though I did not want to leave the university in disgrace. I applied to a couple of opening positions, and received an offer from Western Illinois University, but I ultimately breached the contract with the university. I felt sorry at the time, and I still feel guilty. I later received another offer from Jackson State University in Jackson, Mississippi with higher pay. My reason for accepting this offer was not due to the higher pay, but because Jackson State University was a so-called minority institution of higher education. I was moving out of the South and heading to the Deep South. I was disgusted, and thought I would fare better in a minority institution.

I regret that I was not a humbler person before my colleagues. Dave Hager, the department chairman after Meade, did not like my annual pay protests, and commented that my pay was higher than the president of the Republic of Korea. I responded to him, "You don't know the South Korean president's pay. I don't know it. You and I do not need to know it. I am here. But I know that I deserve a higher pay raise than you guys."

Humility is the indispensable virtue in all human settings, after all. This is how I learned it.

CHAPTER 13

Our Two Children

For the best family reasons, the Tidewater area of Virginia has become "home" — the indispensable place in my life. Our son William was born at Norfolk General Hospital on August 11, 1976 and our daughter Joyce was born a year and a half later at Virginia Beach General Hospital on February 15, 1978. My family became whole here. And so it is our "home" — in the United States and in the world.

I brought my children to the ocean often to let them play with the sand and water. I wanted them to embrace the vast ocean and its constant waves. I also took them often to the farms in the rural areas to be able to appreciate the harvesters' hard work with the soil. Many Americans simply see the produce. They don't know the labor, the sweat and the life of the farm. I grew up on a farm, so I appreciated what the farmers produce.

Before my son's birth, I invited my mother to the United States to help take care of him. It was a good occasion to extend the invitation at that time. My wife was enrolled in the biology program at Old Dominion University, I was teaching full time and my mother and I had been apart for eight full years. My wife had her aspirations and together we worked for her to be able to pursue them. Though she was a pharmacist in Korea, she wanted to take courses in an undergraduate program of the University's Biology Department. If she wanted to work as a pharmacist, she needed a couple of years of additional education in a pharmacy school, and then would need to pass a state board exam to get a license. Since there was no school of pharmacy in the Tidewater area, she enrolled in my university's biology program. My mother accepted the invitation and came to Norfolk to await our newborn boy. Shortly before all this occurred I bought a small house in the Green Run district of Virginia Beach. I had my mother, my newborn son, my wife and myself together living happily in our first house in Virginia Beach.

Our son's birth brought all the happiness in the world to my wife and me. The first baby must be mysterious and miraculous to all parents. He certainly was for us. William was a source of excitement for a long time. I would touch his face, and hold his body, fingers and toes, as I closely and carefully examined his eyes, nose, lips, and hair. His growth offered the family a new happiness over and over again each time we held him. Dr. Mason Andrews, who delivered our son, told me, "Dr. Choi, you have one good healthy boy!" His declaration was a relief.

Babies are like new flowers in March, or chicks, or cubs. They create something new in their parents. It is a new form of happiness. They also create a new responsibility, which is part of the happiness. To experience the joy of becoming a father is to reckon with the happiness and the responsibility together. My wife felt the same joy and excitement.

The above-mentioned doctor who delivered our son, Dr. Mason C. Andrews, was an unusually accomplished man. An OBGYN doctor at Norfolk General Hospital, he was educated and trained at John Hopkins University Medical School, but he also somehow found the time to be elected and then hold the office of Vice Mayor of the city of Norfolk. I met him through a series of public forums I organized at Old Dominion University which were sponsored by the Virginia Foundation for the Humanities and Public Policy. When I met him, I asked him to take care of my pregnant wife and the forthcoming baby. He accepted my request, even though he had stopped seeing new patients due to his research works at Eastern Virginia Medical School. He later became famous for his work with sterile women. When he ran for vice mayor, his election campaign was headed by the memorable "Dr. Andrews delivers!" He sure delivered for us. Even when he wasn't expecting to.

Naming the baby was relatively simple. William J. Choi was his name. He was named after my mentor at Indiana University, William J. Siffin. J was for James in Siffin, but "J" stood for "Jay" in the Choi tradition. My father gave him his Korean name, Jae Chul. Thus, I adapted his middle name to Jay so that William could have both his

American name and a Korean one. I told my mentor Dr. Siffin and he was happy to hear it. Another name was briefly considered: Orion, he of Greek mythology. Orion is a handsome and strong hunter. But we decided against that one in the end. In my American life, William J. Siffin was the most important person, so naming my son after him was more meaningful.

Our son stayed in the hospital for a few more days after his birth because he had jaundice. My mother watched him through the window. Since the hospital did not allow my mother to hold a newborn baby, her joy came a few days later when he was finally discharged. My mother shared a room with him. She felt the baby needed her care 24 hours a day. Meanwhile, my wife was breast-feeding. So the baby was surrounded by his loving mother, grandmother, and father.

Our son was visited by our friends, neighbors, students inside and outside the Tidewater area. Korean parents hold celebrations on the birth, first week, first month, first 100 days, and the first year of a baby's life. Every day for a year is full of happiness. One of my students, a professional photographer, came to our house to take photos after a month. We sent the pictures to our families in Korea. Since I am my father's first son, and he in turn was the first son born to his father, the Choi family's celebration was especially important, and it lasted especially long. Our son was maintaining the family tree for the past 12 + 1 generations.

I wrote a poem to commemorate it entitled, **My Child**, which was published in the *Korea Times* in Los Angeles.

My Child

You are opening your eyes
to the parents,
to the flowers,
to the trees, and
to the ocean
As the wonders.

Life is a kind of wonder:

You are offering
A wonder
To me.

You are playing with musical toys
And you are softly falling into sleep.

Now, I see
My own infant's portrait
From you.
No one remembers his/
her infant look.

Our first outing from Green Run was the Atlantic Ocean;
There you were watching the vast blue waters.
The waves were coming to you.
But you were not afraid of the waves.
You were like a seagull.

Our second outing was the farmer's home;
There you were seeing cows on meadow,
and the farmers working in the field.

The maple tree I planted on the day of your birth
Outside your room
Is growing
Like the gingko tree
My father planted on the day of my birth
In the front yard of our country house.

I hope you grow as the maple tree
To be a man of the strength and beauty
with the farmer's good heart and innocence.

My mother stayed with us for ten months. Those ten months were the happiest time for our family. For my mother's sightseeing pleasure, we often visited the Azalea Gardens, the Atlantic Ocean, North Carolina beaches, and the historical towns of Williamsburg, Jamestown, and Yorktown. She wrote in her diary during much of those ten months, which we found hidden in a chest after her death in 2004, and it recorded that period well. Her diary showed her love for her grandson and her family, but it also showed the 'culture shock' she experienced in a new country. She mentioned new discoveries such as Halloween, Thanksgiving, baby showers, disposable diapers, disposable goods, Color TVs, garage sales, American Indians, and American history. More than anything else, though, her diary showed her immeasurable love for her first grandson. I published it in 2007 under the title of "Mother's Love."

History sometimes has a way of intersecting with the most personal, cherished aspects of our lives. It is not always for the bad. When my mother visited the General Douglas McArthur Memorial Building in downtown Norfolk, she read General McArthur's prayer for his son with fascination. She wrote down "Build Me a Son" in her diary.

This is a woman who had observed the liberation of Korea from Japanese colonial rule in 1945, and the Korean War, and the liberation of South Korea from North Korean communist control in 1953. She personally remembered and appreciated General McArthur's victories during the Korean War and the Pacific War.

Build Me a Son
by General Douglas A. MacArthur

Build me a son, O Lord, who will be strong enough to know when he is weak, and brave enough to face himself when he is afraid; one who will be proud and unbending in honest defeat, and humble and gentle in victory.

Build me a son whose wishbone will not be where his backbone should be; a son who will know Thee....Lead him, I pray, not in the path of ease and comfort, but under the stress and spur of difficulties and challenge. Here let him learn to stand up in the storm; here let him learn compassion for those who fail.

Build me a son whose heart will be clean, whose goal will be high; a son who will master himself before he seeks to master other men; one who will learn to laugh, yet never forget how to weep; one who will reach into the future, yet never forget the past.

And after all these things are his, add, I pray, enough of a sense of humor, so that he may always be serious, yet never take himself too seriously. Give him humility, so that he may always remember the simplicity of greatness, the open mind of true wisdom, the meekness of true strength.

Then I, his father, will dare to whisper, "I have not lived in vain."

* * * * *

My mother took such close care of William that she recorded his every visit to the pediatrician's office for his regular check-ups and immunization shots during her stay. The doctor told her, "Your grandson is the # 1 baby!" She proudly quoted the doctor's statement in her diary. Our baby grew nicely. He liked people around him and was not shy. He was popular among the doctors and nurses. He showed that same unusually developed personality later during his high school days. He was voted president of the English Honor Society and the most popular fellow by his classmates in his high school-days, and the captain of his lacrosse team in college.

Our son, educated and trained at New York University's Stern School of Business, is now working in San Francisco as a fund manager. He is a tall and handsome Orion who married Sarah Kim from Texas in July 2006 at Park City, a satellite town of Salt Lake City, Utah. My life with our son has been a panorama. I read a poem at his wedding reception written for the day. Here is how it goes.

Prayer on Our Son's Wedding

Bless our son leaving our nest!
Let him fly over the high and vast sky
With his strong heart and spirit.
Let him be our son
Who makes this world be a more beautiful habitat.

Our Two Children

With a lovely young woman as his wife,
Let them build their own nest to create
Their own happiness.

May their life be richer and more prosperous than ours!
Let him bring their children into this world
In glorifying the name of our family and our nation.
Let them educate their children to show
Hope and dreams to their neighbors.

Thus, departing our nest will be a new life and a new blessing:
Let him love his one and only sister forever.
Lord, let us be closer and unite us in more affection and admiration,
As our son marries his lovely fiancee.

*With my parents and my youngest sister, Won,
at Kimpo Airport, outside Seoul, in 1967 when
I left for the University of the Philippines.*

*With my friends, Park Ki-Sung, Hong Jin-Il, Hwang Eui-Gak
and my brother, Hyuck, at Kimpo Airport, outside Seoul,
in 1967 when I left for the University of the Philippines.*

My design for Citizens and the Environment Public Forum Series in Mississippi, 1981.

With Kim Dae-jung, exiled dissident leader who
became the president of Korea in 1998 and the
Nobel Peace Prize winner in 2000, at a book party in 1984.

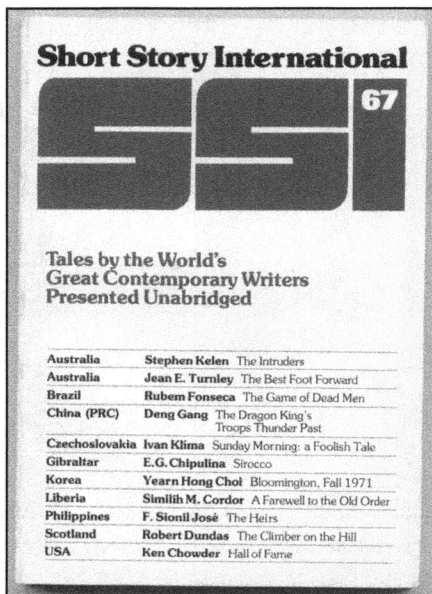

Short Story International

SSI 67

Tales by the World's
Great Contemporary Writers
Presented Unabridged

Australia	Stephen Kelen The Intruders
Australia	Jean E. Turnley The Best Foot Forward
Brazil	Rubem Fonseca The Game of Dead Men
China (PRC)	Deng Gang The Dragon King's Troops Thunder Past
Czechoslovakia	Ivan Klima Sunday Morning: a Foolish Tale
Gibraltar	E.G. Chipulina Sirocco
Korea	Yearn Hong Chol Bloomington, Fall 1971
Liberia	Similih M. Cordor A Farewell to the Old Order
Philippines	F. Sionil José The Heirs
Scotland	Robert Dundas The Climber on the Hill
USA	Ken Chowder Hall of Fame

*My first short story, "Bloomington, Fall 1977" in
Short Story International, early 1980s.*

*Interviewing Reed Whittemore, Poetry Consultant,
for the Library of Congress in the mid-1980s, in his office.*

With Novelist Yong Ik Kim, Amb. Kim Kyung-won, President Sam Kyun Yoon of the Korea Foundation, and President Se-Kwon Chong of the Korean Association at the Smithonian Institutions in the mid-1980s.

With my wife and two children, Jay and Joyce, on New Year's Day in the late-1980s, at home.

*With Allen Ginsberg, Andrei Voznesensky, Russian poet, and Jon Silkin,
British poet at the 1990 World Congress of Poets in Seoul, Korea..*

*With Russian poet Andrei Voznesensky and Poetess Kwak Sang-hee of New York
and an unknown Korean poet at the Korean Arts Center in Seoul, 1990.*

With Kim Young-sam, president-elect of Korea, visiting Washington in 1992. I was introducing Dr. Paik Soon, my friend, to him at the Capital Hilton Hotel Ballroom.

After my first poetry reading at the Library of Congress in 1994. From right to left: Jennifer Rutland, Moon Hee Kim, Chungmi Kim, Dr. Prosser Gifford, myself, and my wife.

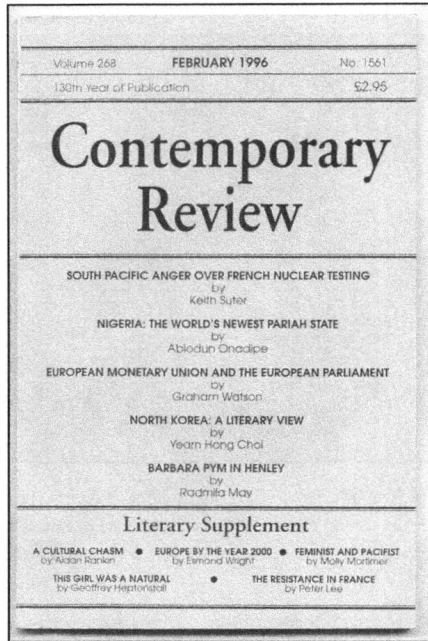

Volume 268　　　**FEBRUARY 1996**　　　No. 1561

130th Year of Publication　　　£2.95

Contemporary Review

SOUTH PACIFIC ANGER OVER FRENCH NUCLEAR TESTING
by
Keith Suter

NIGERIA: THE WORLD'S NEWEST PARIAH STATE
by
Abiodun Onadipe

EUROPEAN MONETARY UNION AND THE EUROPEAN PARLIAMENT
by
Graham Watson

NORTH KOREA: A LITERARY VIEW
by
Yearn Hong Choi

BARBARA PYM IN HENLEY
by
Radmila May

Literary Supplement

A CULTURAL CHASM　●　EUROPE BY THE YEAR 2000　●　FEMINIST AND PACIFIST
by Aidan Rankin　　by Esmond Wright　　by Molly Mortimer

THIS GIRL WAS A NATURAL　　　●　　　THE RESISTANCE IN FRANCE
by Geoffrey Heptonstall　　　　　by Peter Lee

"North Korea: A Literary View," in Comtemporary Review, 1996.

*With Korean-American poets and writers at Kyungju, Korea
in front of Silla Kingdom's tomb, 2002.*

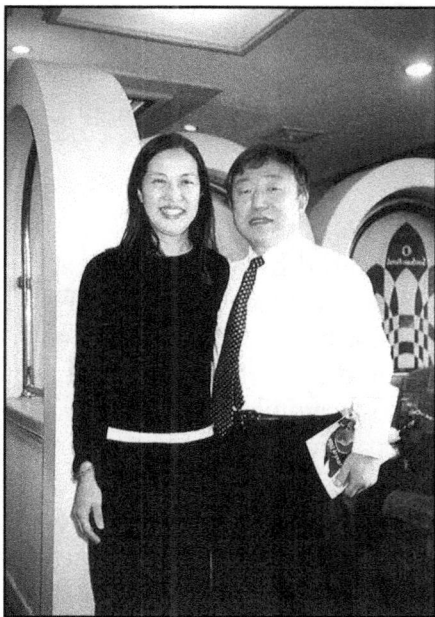

*With Cathy Song who won the Yale Younger Poets Prize
with "Picture Bride" in 1983, at an international
conference at Taegu, Korea in 2002.*

01/17/2003

*After my second poetry reading at the Library of Congress in 2003. From left to right:
Dr. Yoon Soo Park, myself, Dr. Prosser Gifford, Haengja Kim, and Kwi Soon Kwon.*

CHAPTER 14

My Daughter's Arrival

Joyce was born on a chilly February afternoon at the Virginia Beach General Hospital one day before Valentine's Day. For that reason, being my sentimental self, I've always called her my "Valentine girl."

It happens that she was born during the time when I was experiencing the most painful professional agony in my life. The Political Science Department at Old Dominion denied my tenure, which inarguably is the hardest experience any academic must go through professionally. Suddenly, the university became a painful place. The birth of my daughter mitigated my pain inside the university, which was a fine mercy. Joyce was a new hope to me. A daughter is a father's sweetheart. Since February 15, 1978, she has been my sweetheart.

I was already an "old man" when I had a son in August 1976, so our daughter in February 1978 was not only a gift to me, but also to our son. They would not be lonely in this world. They could make life's journey together, comforting each other, embracing each other, and cheering each other on. The Rev. Ji Duk Doh, pastor of the local Korean church, visited the hospital and offered a blessing for my daughter. My change of heart toward God brought new life to me.

We named our daughter Joyce Emily Choi, wishing joy on her life and our family. Without any knowledge of what she would become later in life, we hoped that she would become a writer like Emily Bronte, author of "Wuthering Heights." Like her name, my daughter was happy. She did not cry. My wife and I did not know when she awoke. She would be listening to the music from a musical toy and playing with Winnie the Pooh. She was quite independent. My mother had returned to Seoul in May 1976, so she was alone with her mother and father. She seemed to know our situation. We were grateful to her.

Our baby girl did not draw as much attention as our son from our friends and neighbors, but she offered just as much happiness to us as our son. One Korean friend who had two sons envied me and joked: "Dr. Choi, you have great skill in making a son and a daughter. I should have acquired that skill." We all laughed. Joyce not only offered us laughter, but was also the agent of an important change in my heart. I wrote an essay about it entitled, appropriately, "A Change of Heart," in the *Korea Times* published in Los Angeles:

Immigrants are romanticists. At least, this immigrant is. When an immigrant's romanticism begins to fade, he might search for peace and comfort. After 10 years of life in America and as my romanticism waned, I came to throw myself into the Christian life. Ten years of romanticism might be enough.

Serenity slowly begins to replace romanticism. Then you come to feel that you are tired of foreign life with its struggle, challenges and the discrimination, both visible and invisible, from the establishment. You want now to avoid the fight against obstacles — the majority rule and the establishment's bias and prejudice.

You come to look at your small children. You come to calculate that one plus one is always two. Suddenly you realize you have a limited life. Physically you are tired of the tension of your old life. When you are hospitalized for the first time in your life, you begin to realize the meaning of health and existence that you have never thought of before. Then, if you are like me, you can find that a church, which did not mean very much to you before, now does. The door is always open to you and for you. There you find peace, comfort and serenity.

The other night I was set to make a speech at an American chapel on immigrant and the church. I did not know what to say. Finally, I found an easy way out. That way was to simply disclose my state of mind during my ten years of life as a foreigner — first as a student, then as an immigrant and finally as a naturalized citizen.

"Romanticism is concerned not with the prosaic things but with the poetic joy of discovering beauty wherever it may be found. In landscape, the sea, the sky and the human soul, I tried to discover and touch romanticism. Romanticism does not deny God, but neither does it emphasize Him either. Let's say that Romanticism is closer to a bar than to a church. Wandering is a way of avoiding or attempting to replace worship on Sunday morning. Hard work and tension do not lead to serenity. A person can fall to drinking, to cursing …. and then fever. All the while, I invited more harm to myself.

"Reading the Bible can be a comfort to anyone who is disposed to its message. Classic literature offers some comfort, but not the kind the Bible offers. Shakespeare, Hesse, Hugo, Mansfield, Frost, Hemingway and Steinbeck were my close friends. But they did not offer the same value as the Gospel according to Mark (Chapter 4, Verse 29), which reads:

Jesus stood up and commanded the wind, 'Be quiet!'
And he said to the waves, "Be still!'
The wind died down, and there was great calm.

"The longer you live in another culture, the more you face problems. This brings even more tension and conflict. The higher up you move in the social and occupational hierarchy, the more discrimination you face. Racism is the pernicious doctrine that the people of one race are congenitally superior and that all other races are congenitally inferior. The sin of racism is the sin of despising those for whom Christ died.

"The Gospel of Jesus Christ applies to these areas just as much as it does in such areas of life as prayer, stewardship and Bible study. True Christianity should be color-blind. If this country is truly Christian, we might never have racial injustice and discrimination. The Bible heals the pain from racial bias and prejudice. This, from Exodus (Chapter 23, Verse 9), offers me comfort:

Do not mistreat a foreigner. You know how it feels to be one, because you were foreigners in Egypt.

"Churches act upon Jesus' word to provide comfort, satisfaction and wisdom. You can also simply meet excellent people inside a church. You can find a new kind of romanticism which discovers and pictures, for those of us who would otherwise be inarticulate, the love, the light, the beauty of God so richly incarnate in Jesus Christ.

"Jesus was born in an obscure village. He was the son of a peasant woman. He grew up in another village, and that a despised one. He worked in a carpenter shop for 30 years. He was an itinerant preacher. He never wrote a book. He never held an office. He never owned a home. He never had a family. He never went to college. He had no credentials but Himself."

This was my speech at the American chapel, and it was well received by my American neighbors. The above reflected my state of mind in 1978. My daughter, just born, drew it out of me. She was the agent for me to believe in God. Marjorie Mitchell, my old friend and neighbor in the Larchmont apartment in Norfolk, presented her own Good News Bible to me as a gift. That was my first Bible in English. I still keep it as my treasure on my bookshelf. I discovered Love in 1 Corinthian (Chapter 13, Verses 4 through 7). I read it everyday since then:

Love is patient and kind; it is not jealous or conceited or proud; love is not ill-mannered or selfish or irritable; love does not keep a record of wrongs; love is not happy with evil, but it is happy with the truth. Love never gives up; and its faith, hope, and patience never fail.

Joyce made us happy. As a little girl, she questioned everything. "Why is the sky blue?" and "Why are there four seasons?" even before she went to elementary school. I could not answer her questions well. During her high school days, she was a reader and editor of my articles, poems and essays including my weekly *Korea Herald* column, "Washington Perspective," over a long period of 1987-1993. During her college days, she spent one semester in Paris and one summer as an intern at the French Central Bank. While she was in Paris, I wrote a poem, "Joyce in Paris."

Daughter — Joyce in Paris

Even though you are a thousand miles away,
You are always within me:
The peaceful baby's sleep
Born after Valentine's Day,

A gifted school girl's brilliance and
A young lady's charm
Constitute your highness.
You are the best present from God to us.

Even though you are a thousand miles away,
You are breathing in my forest:
You are sending good news like a morning magpie.
You are constant comfort like flowers.
Your voice on the overseas call
Is like whispers of a lark.

Even though you are a thousand miles away,
You are the brilliant star in our night sky:
Each word in your letter is
Descending to the Earth from sky.
Oh, I now realize, "A daughter is daddy's sweetheart."

Vitality, joy, happiness
Every father has
Come from the daughter's beautiful postcard.
Your letters warm and brighten the cold winter.
Your presence makes this world
So beautiful:
A divine communication between the two continents.
A powerful prose runs into a verse,
A breath in our lives.

After college, Joyce worked for Morgan Stanley in New York City and its Hong Kong office. She rose to be Vice President of the organization. Now, she is working for Tudor, an investment company in Connecticut. She has been sending me the *New Yorker* as my weekly reading. I thank her for lovely gifts on my birthday from New York City. I am proud of her. I dedicated my most recent poetry book, *Moon of New York*, to her.

Moon of New York

A great night scene is New York City
From the 86th floor of the Empire State Building
At nine,
But the greatest night scene is New York City
With a full moon, viewed from Hamilton Park
In New Jersey,
The same moon that the coyote howled at in the Arizona desert.
The moon on the left corner of the night
Is reflected on the Hudson River,
While making black and white waves
Toward the Atlantic.
My daughter is sleeping in an apartment
In midtown Manhattan.
Beethoven's Moonlight Sonata is still flowing.
It is Thanksgiving Night.

CHAPTER 15

My U.S. Citizenship and a Woman's Death

Soon after my son was born I became a naturalized citizen. In the citizenship ceremony at Norfolk Court House, I met a Korean woman who became a naturalized citizen at the same time when I became one. Before I left Virginia for Mississippi, I read a sad article from the *Virginian-Pilot* about her death. I was shocked to hear about it, especially how it occurred. It prompted me to write her story. It was inspired by my shock over what happened to her.

* * * * *

A Woman's Death

I don't know what is really with me; uncomfortable, uneasy, or guilty. She was killed by her husband after they had separated. Her husband was a U.S. sailor. He killed himself after he had killed his estranged wife in their bedroom. The Norfolk Daily newspaper called them "estranged." They were 35. Their young daughters were adopted by her sister and sent to Korea. That tragedy happened on the first week of September in 1976. But I still cannot clearly stop feeling some discomfort from her death. Probably ten years from now, I will still have some uncomfortable, uneasy, or guilty feeling. I may carry this discomfort to my tomb.

I knew of her, but I didn't know her very well personally. It was more through the Korean-American grapevine in the town. The grapevine accentuated the fact that her husband was a Navy cook, and that he was a native of the Philippines. I had met her family, the husband and two children. I also saw her two oil paintings hanging on the living room wall of one of my close friends. The paintings proved her to be an artist, yes, but I am not an art critic. I myself didn't know or couldn't tell whether she was a professional artist or whether she had potential to be a great artist.

I still do not fully understand why an artist married a cook, a Filipino cook in the U.S. Navy. Any marriage is only understandable on its own terms. An artist can marry a convict. A cook can marry a millionaire heiress. But to most Koreans, a marriage between artist and cook was not acceptable or even possible. After I met her family, I could understand their marriage better. They came to attend the Korean-American Musical Concert at Chrysler Hall in June of that year. She introduced her husband and children. He was a handsome man. I could instantly see that he was a nice and mild person.

"You are a handsome man. You should go to Hollywood." He was so shy that he did not say anything to me other than a smile. She whispered to me, "Because of you, we came here."

Because I was president of the Korean-American Association of the Norfolk metropolitan area, which sponsored the concert, she and her family had come. The musical concert was not the primary reason for their coming. I was thinking this in a confused and uncomfortable way.

I interpreted her whispering as a light joke. It was the best way. Sonja was a beautiful woman. A beautiful woman chose a handsome man from an Asian country. When they married, they might have been in their early twenties. They could have seen in each other a desirable youth and beauty, rather than fame or wealth. Sexual curiosity would also have played a role in their decision to get married. Then, too, a marriage between a Filipino man and a Korean woman could be considered less international or foreign when compared to a marriage between a Korean woman and an American or German man. Hailing from Asia could make the two close enough to be at least somewhat comfortable together in the United States.

They had lived in San Diego and San Francisco before coming to Norfolk. They were happily married when they moved to Norfolk. Sonja's husband confided their happy marriage to Hahn, their neighbor and my close friend. He often visited Hahn's house, just across the street, after she left for Richmond to do graduate study in art during the summer of that year.

She had received her bachelor's degree in art from a small private college in Norfolk in May. Then she filed for divorce. The couple was separated in distance when she left for Richmond. I heard all of this through Hahn.

Her college degree had already separated the couple. A college degree can separate a person from navy cook, I thought. What had made her decide to go to college? The town's Korean community might have stirred up her Korean consciousness. That is my guess. If they had stayed on the West Coast, they would not have experienced separation and the events that led to such a tragic death. If he had been a medical doctor or engineer, their marriage might have continued as it had been. Korean society in Norfolk reflected the old Korean caste system. It's at least partially to blame.

* * * * *

Hahn once asked me, "Why did she marry a Filipino?"

I laughed. "What's the matter with you? She married a nice person." I was a single man. But I was not interested in her romantically. Often I enjoyed her piano rhythm when I visited Hahn's home.

"She likes your column. She never misses your column," Hahn told me. My column appeared twice a week, Wednesday and Friday, in a Korean language newspaper based in Washington, D.C.

To be honest, I had curiosity about her from the grapevine, but after I met her family, I felt no more questions or curiosity.

There was a link in this curiosity that went like this: It was in May at the Norfolk District Court. I was there to get my U.S. citizenship. I had made a petition for my citizenship almost a year before. Prior to the official ceremony, all the citizens-to-be gathered to make a final check with a form that contained a few questions such as: "Have you committed a crime since you filed the petition?" or, "Have you been arrested since you filed the petition?"

A Korean lady approached me and asked me about one of the questions on the form. I suggested that she check the "no" column. She was not confident with her English. As the judge called every petitioner's name, his or her occupation, and home country, he introduced her as Sonja, a freelance artist from the Republic of Korea. I was a bit surprised to know her in that way. She was so attractive. I could understand why I had heard of her in the Korean-American grapevine for so long.

I wanted to keep my U.S. citizenship a secret to the world until I was accustomed to it. Giving up one's home country's citizenship may not be one's proudest achievement. Certainly, it was a betrayal to the home country.

I enjoyed Bedrich Smetana's "My Country," the Czech composer whose piece conjures up the spirit of Bohemia, its history and traditions. I am still enjoying his music. But since Sonja was the first person who knew my changing status among the Korean-Americans, the Koreans in Norfolk knew my citizenship in a few days.

* * * * *

School was over. Summer vacation was underway. About that time, I was admitted to the hospital to have a medical check up. My doctor could not understand why I was often sick with a high fever and a sore throat. While I was lying in the hospital room, I got a call from Sonja.

"Dr. Kim, what's the matter with you? Why is such a young man like you hospitalized? Do you know why you are sick? Because you are single. Some girl should take care of you. You need a girl. You should change your marital status soon."

I complained: "That is not a very friendly way to greet a friend in a hospital. You better visit me in person. You know what? When you kiss me, I'll be O.K." I joked somewhat uneasily.

We both laughed. I still felt uncomfortable, but was sure she would not come.

Unexpectedly, to say the least, she came to visit me the next day with chrysanthemums. But she did not know what to say. She was shy and her face was red. Trying to put her at ease, I opened our conservation with Vincent van Gogh's works. Van Gogh's "Empty Chair" was my first poem published in the most prestigious poetry magazine in my college days. Van Gogh was and is still the most unforgettable painter to me. I explained the Empty Chair with handkerchief and pipe. His sad and tragic life itself is poetic. His passionate intensity is contrary to the tragic life. We discussed "The Church at Anvers," "Self-Portrait with a Gray Hat," "The Potato Eaters," and "Paul Gauguin." This artist who had shot himself drew out our sympathy and compassion.

I found her to be a knowledgeable person about art as we talked. I could see her knowledge was more than just surface-level. She talked about Van Gogh's influence on Fauvism and German Expressionism. She was much engrossed in Kandinsky's Blue Rider's group in München. The blue horse was a symbol of Kandinsky and his sweetheart, Gabriel Munter, and other artists before World War I.

Out of our conversation, we found we had a mutual friend from our high school days. She was a graduate of K girls' high school in Seoul. We were graduates of the year of 1959. Sook, my friend in a poetry club in high school days, had been Sonja's close friend. Two girls in poetry and art could be close in that age.

She was more comfortable with me after we had found a common ground in the year of 1959. She was nostalgic about her high school days. Of course, thinking about the past is almost always more beautiful than it actually was. Aging makes us think back to adolescent days when almost everyone has dreams and hopes. Youth is ever chasing after the rainbow. We talked easily of several things, and then Sonja spoke to me of my newspaper columns. She told me: "Your essays are often personal. Why do you expose your inner self to your readers? Are you paid well for your exposure? Aren't you scared? You are too honest. I don't like such a person. I wouldn't like you to write anything about me. Never!"

"Writers and artists should expose their ideas and thoughts to the readers. That is why they are paid. You just use color, and I use words. That's the only difference."

She grimaced. "I have to be careful."

She was starting to leave my room.

I told her, "I'm not O.K. if you don't kiss me." I felt much more at ease with her now, even to this point of boldness.

But her face turned red again. She left me without a kiss.

It was after this hospital episode that I met her with her family at the Chrysler Hall in June, as I described.

* * * * *

The next communication with Sonja was her call from Richmond. I was stunned somewhat as I asked, "Why are you there?"

She just asked me to come at once with: "I have something to talk." I went to Richmond the next Saturday morning. A drive of two hours was not that long to see an old friend. But I was uncomfortable since I was not given an opportunity to reject her request.

Her apartment was near the university.

She greeted me alone.

She explained to me she had decided to pursue an advanced degree in fine arts in Richmond because there was no graduate program offered in the Norfolk area. She might have gone to North Carolina, she said, if Richmond hadn't accepted her.

She showed her burning ambition to be an artist, a great artist. She already had a plan to open her one-person show in Richmond in the fall or winter. She showed me her new happiness in the new town by her glowing descriptions. She told me that her professors liked her works and were encouraging her. I just listened to her. I didn't know what to say. She had treated me as an old friend. She tried to act as my older sister, although she was only one year older than me. But I was, somehow strangely, not comfortable in her apartment. Two persons like us alone in an apartment made me feel absurdly uncomfortable.

When she prepared supper at five, I was more uneasy, more so after the meal. She was a good cook. All Korean women are well trained to be good cooking housewives. We went out for a walk, trying to act as high school classmates to each other.

I said "good-by" about nine that evening. I thought I must go. My place was Norfolk, not in Richmond.

She showed her tears when I left her. I kissed her somewhat impersonally on her cheek. She still stood there in the same spot as I started out of the apartment parking lot. I could not drive away. I could only return to her. I took her to her apartment and said another "good-by." Then, she stopped me.

"Young (Yearn), I'm separated. I'll be divorced. You can stay here with me, if you are not scared of me."

"I'm not scared of you."

She was lonely. Loneliness in her mid-thirties was deep and heavy.

In early August, she called me from Richmond. "I may face a tragedy," she told me. But she showed me her burning ambition and plan, to be an artist, in her voice. She was speaking in a fast tempo.

That was our last conversation.

Two or three minutes' talk at the court house, five minutes' talk to her and her husband at Chrysler Hall, one hour in a hospital room, one day and one night in Richmond, and two telephone conversations were all my relationships with her. However, less than 48 hours with her seemed more than the four years and eight months that I have actually known her.

In early September, she was killed. She had come down to Norfolk to see her children. The sailor killed her and then killed himself.

* * * * *

I have reflected that the cause of such a tragedy was her Korean conscience, or her Korean friends, wives of college professors, of engineers, and of medical doctors.

These women were all graduated from K Girls' High School in Seoul, Korea. They were very proud of their high school because only the most intellectual girls could be admitted to that school. Her friends accepted her as an equal. But they did not accept her husband in their inner circle. That might have been a high liability. I knew of their belief that K school graduates shouldn't marry a cook or a sailor or a Filipino. Sonja was partially accepted and partially rejected. They could almost accuse her by asking: "How come you married such a man? Shame on you!"

It is my guess that these pressures caused her to return to college for her degree, then pursue her advanced degree, and finally to divorce from the sailor.

Korea has been a caste society. Learned subjects were only for the elite or high class in the Yi dynasty. Learned citizens, college degrees, and college professors have been most respected. Korea's economic development now has changed people's attitude toward a kind of pragmatism. Income now turns out to be a key to high social class. In the United States, the pre-1970's Korean generation maintained and kept that old caste system. They didn't see that money could buy the First Lady, or even perhaps, Hollywood's beautiful actresses. They still maintained the values they had held when they left Korea in the 1960s.

A sailor's income might be the same or more than a college teacher's income. Rank is a necessary evil in military organization. But rank outside in society can harm greatly.

She was killed by a Korean disease, a virus of old, an outdated caste system. It is tragic to say it.

Even though the Korean women around her killed her indirectly, I could not clean up my guilty feeling. I still cannot wash it out. I think I am one of the killers.

If I hadn't visited her apartment in Richmond, or if I hadn't told her to see me in the hospital, she might be alive today.

I should have told her in her apartment: "Sonja, what's the matter with you? You should be happy with your husband and children at home. They are beautiful. He is a nice person. Happiness is not all just your artwork. Happiness is in your heart. There is no guarantee of happiness when you become an artist, even a great artist. Please go home!"

I held these words back. I should have spoken. If I had, this guilt may have not welled up in me. It may not have been as great.

We were not lovers. We didn't think about each other as lovers. We were trying to find friendship from each other in a lonely world. Perhaps I failed in my imagination to return to high school days while she succeeded. I still do not know that we had a really common nostalgia in our short friendship. I miss my life before I left Korea in 1967. Our life style was quite primitive, but we were happy. We all considered ourselves as the products of 1960s.

When she was killed, her friends from K Girls' High School accused her husband immediately. I just listened to them. I almost shouted to them: "Shut up! You are the murderers!" I still cannot call him a murderer, because the man whose hand I shook in Chrysler Hall was not a killer. I have never felt that he was the killer.

The Korean women said to each other. "He should kill himself if he wanted. Why kill her?"

They didn't understand why he killed her. They never tried to understand him. He loved her that much. He couldn't erase fifteen years of happy life with her. He could only bury that happiness with her.

* * * * *

Friendship contains a piece of love.

I have visited Hahn since. And her paintings are still hung on his living room wall. An oil painting, a seascape, is too much blue. Blue is scary to me. I didn't like that painting before her death. I still don't like it today. But I do not ask Hahn to remove the painting. I do not have any intention to ask him to do so. I don't have any right to ask. I don't want anybody to discover our friendship or love, whichever it may have been.

I remember her as a blue woman. I have considered her as a blue woman after:

Makoto Ooka's poem, "Blue Women."

Candies and pastries come in many different colors, but blue, I am certain, is the one used least.

Something holds us back from biting into a pastry of midnight blue or devouring a candy as blue as the clearest ocean. Flesh intuits the meaning behind the common image of blue as a cold color.

My beloved Kandinsky said, "Blue is the most celestial of all colors." Yellow, a warm color, is, by contrast, the earthiest.

"Blue increases thickness, increases depth, and so invites man to the infinite and awakens in him a longing for the pure and then the transcendent."

And so, blue is almost never used for sweets. They are too delicious, too earthly, too intimately connected with fleshly joy.

Scoop up the ocean, soar through the sky — no matter how far You go, you can't touch their brimming blue. Water's transparent; so is the sky.

Blue: a color without peer, beyond reality. Because it is the Color of light. The Blue flower, the Bluebird: the color of longing, Of an absent bird.

Such women, where are you?

* * * * *

I avoid visiting Hahn in his home as much as possible.

CHAPTER 16

Mississippi, My Magnolia State

It was time to depart. So I gave some of my books and some furniture to my students and friends as Christmas gifts. Then we packed our essential items and gave them to the moving company to transport to Jackson, Mississippi. I asked one real estate agent to rent the house or sell the house on an acceptable condition. 1979 was not a good year for home sales. Under President Jimmy Carter, the U.S. economy was struggling with high inflation and high unemployment. Our agent could not even rent the house before we left for Jackson, Mississippi.

We left for Mississippi early one morning in August 1979. Moving under the present circumstances was not pleasant at all. Most probably moving is unpleasant to all people under any circumstances, if you have the house for sale, and if you have to pack so many things. Our moving from Wisconsin to Virginia in 1973 had not been bad at all. Everything fit inside our car in the trunk and backseat. Fortunately, our two young children did not know the sorrow of moving. I just felt sorry for my wife. She was preparing the move as if it were a scientific endeavor. Our hearts were heavy because we could not sell the house before we left. But my father's first letter comforted me again. "Everywhere you go, there will be green mountains!"

Mississippi is known as the Magnolia State. I could already imagine the magnolia flowers in the tall magnolia trees in the front and back yard of the ante-bellum mansions. Mississippi is the land of cotton fields, and in my imagination it also remained the land of sorrow of Black slaves. Mississippi means "the Great Water," or the father of waters, in the language of the Indians who lived in the region in early times. I love the name Mississippi. All Indian names are beautiful. Niagara is "thunder" in the Indian language. I love another Indian name, Kankakee, a town in Illinois I once visited. Mississippi is still to me the place of William Faulkner and Eudora

Welty. I was thinking all good, beautiful things in Mississippi on the way to Jackson, Mississippi. I comforted my wife in despair.

I took the highway to Durham, Charlotte, Atlanta, Birmingham, and Meridian. We stayed the first night in the outskirts of Atlanta. The hotel we stayed in was a lodging place for the Atlanta Falcons, who were preparing for their pre-season games. They adored our two children. I thanked them. I could reach Jackson before the second night fell, but stopped at the small town of Meridian, so that I could touch down at Jackson in the next morning. The following morning, we arrived at the apartment and settled. We found an apartment not very far from the university. Leslie McLemore, the department chairman, arranged for my family to stay there for a year.

Then, I visited Jackson State University. The master of public administration program I belonged to was housed in the political science department, one of the oldest buildings on campus. The University was founded in 1877. The political science building was a wooden building. My office was on the second floor. The floor made noise whenever I stepped. It was no doubt a historic building to be conserved, but it was in pitiful shape. The location of the university and the master's program of public administration were positives because Jackson was the state capital. The University of Mississippi and Mississippi State University were far from the center of the state. But, interestingly, the MPA Program at the State Capital did not attract many white students — more on that later.

* * * * *

Jackson has been the state capital since 1821 when the Mississippi legislature established the capital in the center of the state at a site called Le Fleur's Bluff. The legislature named the site Jackson to honor Major General Andrew Jackson, hero of the War of 1812 and later President of the United States. When I studied public administration at Yonsei University in Seoul, Korea, I read Leonard D. White's classics including "Jacksonian Democracy." President Jackson, who was from a humble family, adopted a popular political slogan, "Let the People rule!" It has been described as the years of the "rise of the common man" like him, born in a log cabin before Abraham Lincoln's time. I was fascinated when I first learned of Jacksonian

Democracy — the reforms and reform movements from 1828 to 1850 that set the stage for the formation of Abraham Lincoln's Republican Party in 1854.

I took off my jacket and put it on my chair when I went up to my office. And then I went downstairs to meet McLemore. When I returned to my office, my wallet was stolen by an unknown person. It was never returned to me. I made a new Mississippi driver's license and Visa card. Of course, the cash was gone. Dr. McLemore lent me some money and warned me that I should not leave my office unlocked. He told me, "This is a poor university. So you should defend your money." He was honest at least. For a while, I regretted my decision to come to Jackson State University over Western Illinois University. My wife blamed me for my carelessness. I learned a lesson from my first day in the new office.

Without a driver's license, I drove a short distance to my apartment. The apartment's swimming pool was the only place I enjoyed that summer with our two children.

A few days later, the moving truck brought our furniture. We were settling down and things were returning to normal. My wife got her first hospital lab job. Since my teaching was scheduled in three evening classes, I was one happy baby-sitter for our children. I took them to McDonald's, Pizza Hut, Baskin Robbins, the swimming pool, the library, the zoo and the botanical garden, and the Old State Capitol, which housed the state Historical Museum, the State Museum of Natural Science, and Jackson Municipal Art Gallery. My young daughter started to ask many difficult questions: Why do the stars shine in the night sky? Just as she had earlier. It struck me in that Mississippi swimming pool. I didn't have very good answers for her. I realized that she was unusually smart.

Our long-awaited visit to New Orleans happened on one weekend in the first part of October. It was still hot, but a very dry heat. New Orleans is located on the Mississippi Gulf Coast, but it is part of Louisiana. The city always attracted many tourists from foreign countries, especially from South America. During our Mississippi stay we visited New Orleans once more with my uncle from San Francisco. The city impressed him. The French Quarter, jazz music, seafood, shrimp in particular, the Saints football stadium near the water and the old French houses and streets were good enough to attract many tourists.

In 2005, Hurricane Katrina destroyed the city, and reduced the population by half. But I still remember the old New Orleans, our favorite visiting spot, and hope that one day it will return to normal.

On the way to New Orleans, we stopped by Jefferson Davis' home, Beauvoir. Not many people know who this is. Davis was the president of the South during the Civil War. He became president in Richmond, Virginia, and then later was a prisoner of war held by the Union Army. He was confined to a room in Fort Monroe, Hampton, Virginia. I knew his name and life. I was lecturing my MPA students at Ft. Monroe once a week as part of my teaching load at Old Dominion University. His prison cell was next door to my lecture room. So I drove my car to Beauvoir, which was his boyhood home and a historic museum in Biloxi.

The Louisiana Purchase made by President Thomas Jefferson expanded the United States territory all the way north to the Midwestern states. These were the sorts of questions and subjects I thought about as I went to New Orleans! Everything had a historic meaning to me and to my guests.

* * * * *

At Jackson State University, I was in charge of the environmental policy program, and conducted a series of public forums on a possible radioactive waste disposal site in the State of Mississippi, under the sponsorship of the Mississippi Committee for the Humanities. Salt Dome was one possible site for low-level waste. But a radioactive waste disposal site was not welcome by any community. Fear of radioactive waste was and is still enormous. President George W. Bush finally designated Yucca Mountain, the volcanic rock mountain in Nevada for the disposal site, but there is a long way to go to construct the site. Every presidential candidate expressed his or her denial of the Yucca Mountain site. As long as the nation uses and needs nuclear power, X-rays in the hospital, and the like, a radioactive waste disposal site is absolutely necessary. I gave an impression to the Mississippi residents that I was in favor of a radioactive waste disposal site in

Mississippi. I often appeared in the television news at prime time. I was a controversial person from Korea.

One unforgettable experience in my short Mississippi stay was Leslie McLemore's 1980 congressional campaign. He lost to his Republican opponent Trent Lott. Lott became a prominent congressmen and later senator succeeding John Stennis, and the Senate Majority Leader. I was knocking on the doors of each house, asking the people to vote for McLemore. Back then, the line between white and black was very clear. Jackson has a sizable black population, but the white majority voted for Lott. Lott handily won the election.

One summer, I participated in a National Institutes of Health research team investigating sodium content and hypertension in the area. I used data from the University of Mississippi Medical School, and published the negative correlations between sodium content in drinking water and hypertension in the Jackson, Mississippi area in *Environmental Conservation*, one of the best journals in the environmental field from Geneva, Switzerland. Groundwater in the Jackson metropolitan area had high levels of sodium. So I used the data of the people drinking the groundwater in the area. I spent one summer at the medical school. It was a fruitful part of my research, though tragically it was only possible thanks to the misfortune of Mississippi.

In our second year in Mississippi, we sold our Virginia Beach house, although we were forced to do so below the market value. It was ruined by a wild renter and by Jimmy Carter's miserable economic policy. But we moved on, and we built a house in Clinton, a small city next to Jackson. When we celebrated the new home, a couple of our friends told us, "If you build a beautiful house like this one, then you leave this house soon!" Their mythical-sounding forecast would soon prove true.

I was then selected as a National Association of Schools of Public Affairs and Administration Fellow for the 1981-82 academic year. The NASPAA selected professors teaching in the graduate programs of public policy and administration to the U.S. Government under the Intergovernmental Personnel Act for their contributions. The Government selected 10 Fellows. I was one. My selection offered me a working experience in the Office of the Secretary of Defense as an assistant for environmental quality. I had to leave the beautiful house in the wooded hill area, and could not return to that house, as my friends worried.

While in Mississippi, I met Eudora Welty, a famous writer living in Jackson, at her house that her father had built. She was born in Jackson and spent most of her life there. She was the very personification of Jackson to me. She was nice and generous to this Korean poet and writer. She spent almost one hour with me, talking about her life and literature in the South. She was still shy at her old age in her seventies. Her first short story, "Death of a Traveling Salesman," appeared in 1936, in which she emphasized the value of family. Her first collection of short stories, "A Curtain of Green," was published in 1941, in the year I was born. Her novel "The Optimist's Daughter" won the Pulitzer Prize in 1973. She was known as the best short story writer of her time. She was still an active writer when I met her.

I did not find time to visit Faulkner's house in Oxford as I wanted to, as my two years in Mississippi were quickly gone like the wind.

* * * * *

In Jackson, Mississippi, I met one sad and unfortunate woman from Korea. I can never forget the woman. One day I received a telephone call from the court in the city of Jackson. The court needed an interpreter for a Korean woman who had been raped and almost killed several months before. The court official told me that he had a hard time finding an interpreter for the Korean language in the town. Not many Korean people lived in the city.

The Korean woman needed my sympathy and compassion. She married a U.S. soldier stationed in Korea and had a daughter. When she came to Jackson, her husband's hometown, he abandoned her. She maintained two menial jobs to support herself and her infant daughter. Her mother-in-law was doing the baby-sitting. When she was attacked, she was on the way to pick up her daughter in the late night. After the attacker raped her and nearly choked her to death, she lost consciousness for many hours. In the morning, she was sent to a hospital emergency room. She survived.

Her neck was still bruised in red with the finger prints. The merciless attacker tried to kill her in order to erase any evidence of the criminal act. In order to erase one criminal act, he left more serious evidence of crime over her neck. I could not control my anger for this criminal when I first saw her.

The alleged killer was accompanied by a public defender, who represented him. The United States was unbelievably a great country, I thought, if it pays for the defense with taxpayers' money. The lawyer's questions were more than cruel to my ears. He asked a question to her: "How can you point out him as the rapist?" Her answer was: "I could clearly see him, and see him, because he raped me and tried to kill me." He responded: "It was so dark. Midnight. How could you see him in darkness? There was a dim street light in distance."

I could not believe the lawyer's questions and comments for the merciless criminal.

His fingerprints on her neck should be sufficient evidence to convict him, I thought. It was 1979 and there was no such thing yet as DNA evidence in common usage. What made me angry was from the lawyer's following question:

"Were you looking for a man that night?"

Her response was: "I was on the way to pick up my baby."

The lawyer responded to her with a conviction: "No. It is an excuse. You are a young woman who needs sex!"

I invited her to a very small Korean church in Jackson. I wish she would find at least one comfortable place of refuge, inside that church.

No one can forget a woman in such a tragedy in Mississippi.

CHAPTER 17

Pentagon Duty

There was a long background check before I could report to the Pentagon. Being a naturalized citizen from Korea, the investigative process for me would be considerably more extensive than the average candidate. As I filed my papers in preparation, I made sure to let my Pentagon investigators know that I had been a poet and writer who opposed South Korea's authoritarian regime and for that reason had regularly received North Korean propaganda in the mail. I did not know how, but I guessed that my anti-South Korean government writings were being interpreted in Pyongyang as pro-North Korean writings! I also received propaganda regularly from around the Communist bloc: Havana, Cuba, Wien, Austria, Budapest, Hungary, and Prague, Czechoslovakia. I very clearly was part of North Korea's mailing list on the idea that if a person opposes one regime, they must support its enemy.

Fortunately, my Pentagon investigators weren't so obtuse. In America, there is room to criticize South Korea's authoritarian regime on grounds of principle but also oppose even more the "animal farm" of North Korea under dictator Kim Il-sung. I could show a record of declining involvement with the Communist bloc when presented with the opportunity. In the 1970s, for instance, I was once invited to a conference on Korea's unification in Wien or Helsinki. I never accepted the invitation, because I knew I could not express fair or neutral views at North Korea-sponsored conferences.

But for reasons such as these contacts my investigation took a long time. When it finally came, I was granted access to deal with secret government documents, but not top-secret level documents, because my job at the Pentagon required only secret-level clearance. I reported for duty to the Pentagon in the morning of October 1, 1981.

* * * * *

As a scholar of public administration and a naturalized citizen, the Pentagon job was a privilege. I thanked the United States. This must be the only nation in the world that could offer an opportunity to work in the Office of the Secretary of Defense to a foreign-born citizen. When I arrived at the Pentagon Metro Station, I slowly walked to the gate, and I called Dr. Don Emig inside.

Emig was my boss who interviewed me a couple of times over the phone, and was the person who offered me the fellowship. He came out to the gate to pick me up. That was our first meeting. That was my first entrance into the Pentagon, and the first step toward my two years sojourn there. It was my best opportunity to see environmental policy and management inside the government. Two years inside the bureaucracy enriched my teaching and research works.

Don Emig was a tall and handsome man who earned his doctorate degree in environmental engineering from Purdue University. He introduced me to his staff, an air force lieutenant colonel and a navy officer with a secretary. Immediately, he assigned me to look into the documents stored in the cabinet for a week, and to handle Department of Defense's low-level nuclear waste papers from a perspective of the newly enacted law in the Radioactive Waste Policy Act of 1980. The U.S. Congress passed a law for low-level radioactive waste policy just before Christmas that did not mention the Department of Defense (DOD) waste at all. The law urged inter-state compacts for waste management. My job was to make DOD a part of these interstate compacts, and to ensure that these compacts would accept DOD waste. The problem, of course, was that each state feared hosting Pentagon waste. Low-level radioactive waste of 10 nano curies is the same regardless of who produced it. But state politicians and bureaucrats were thinking the DOD waste was more harmful than the electric utility's waste. So I became the liaison between the DOD and the 50 State Governments over their interstate compacts.

In a new town, I enjoyed reading the *Washington Post* every morning, and discovered the Sunday's Outlook section had an outsider's essay entitled "Company Town: A personal glimpse of Washington." I composed an essay and mailed it to the *Post*. The

editor called me and informed me that a photographer would visit my office for a photo. What an honor to place my essay with my photo. It was printed on November 1, 1981.

I reprint it here in this space, because it was a most delightful essay that appeared in the most respectable national newspaper. But also because it shows how I was adapting to my new job at the time.

Scholar-Bureaucrat in a Town of Transition

Monday

I report to duty, but cannot enter the Pentagon Building because the guards stop me. I call the director of environmental policy inside and he "rescues" me.

I was chosen for a Defense Department faculty fellow to acquire experience from the practical world for the university and public administration profession. Meeting with a personnel administrator is a good experience; he explains the focus of the office in the Defense Department. Long-range goals and major functions of the office are rather new to me, because I taught broad environmental policy and administration. The boss gives me "homework" to be done in a week, to review all the memorandums in the file cabinet.

The Defense Department was assigned to investigate regional waste management feasibility with other federal, state and local government agencies. Fourteen reports were made by the Defense Department; reviewing the files is educational.

Tuesday

During lunch hour, I go out to find an apartment, my nest. One apartment at Roslyn is known well as an "easy place" to get in. From the Pentagon office to Roslyn is like a long tunnel, or cave, except for about a mile near the Arlington Cemetery station.

A young lady in the rental office explains the necessary procedures to get in. Security clearance is ubiquitous. The Defense Department took more than two months to investigate my background — ideas, family, education and career. Now an old apartment wants my personal and financial backgrounds.

"Are you really from Mississippi?" she asks me. "Yes," I answer, "I am." Mississippi may be out of the United States, or maybe I don't look like a Mississippian.

I review about 100 pages from the file; that is more than I usually read at the university.

Wednesday

I meet a friend, a special project director of an educational television station, who once invited me to serve as an advisory member to the project. She is doing "Spaces," half-hour science programs designed to encourage minority students ages 9-13 to consider science and technology-related professions as career choices and to highlight the accomplishments of minority scientists. We discuss the relationship of science and technology. Science policymakers are saying that technology is behind science, mainly due to the fact that scientists don't like to be identified with technologists. President Reagan's economic recovery plan should reduce the gap between the two.

Washington seems to me a town for the ambitious, always transitional from one president to another, from one congressman to another, from a congressmen's secretary who does not know how to type to another.

Thursday

The boss invites me to dinner and to stay overnight at his home. He is a commuter from suburban Baltimore with several others from the Pentagon and other government agencies. His family is kind and hospitable. The Asians are not the only hospitable people in the world. His wife is of Italian descent, and dinner was Italian. We recollect our happy days and our unhappy days — his Vietnam days and my early immigrant days.

Friday

We get up at 5AM. My friend's wife already has prepared breakfast. At 5:30, we leave Bel Air. On the way to work, most men continue their morning sleep in the van. It is still dark when we arrive at the Pentagon. We start to work at 7. I realize that the boss has been working more than 10 hours a day. We should really evaluate the performance of government employees fairly. I don't dispute the fact that there have been many incompetent, lousy workers. I just wonder whether there are more lousy government employees than outside the government world.

In the afternoon, I present a 10-page report to the director which contains a review of the Solid Waste Disposal Act as amended by the Resource Recovery Act and by the Resource Conservation and Recovery Act, 14 regional studies and my recommendations on what steps the Defense Department should take. Solid waste management is completely forgotten by the government leaders and citizens, because hazardous and nuclear wastes have emerged as the more dangerous products.

Saturday

I write an epilogue for my book. A week inside the government helped me write it. Here is part of it: "Being a member of an organization is like belonging to an orchestra whose sole aim is to comprise a harmonious assembly for the performance of music. In such an organization, each one's functions contribute to the total effect of the performance. There springs a faith among the members that each is indispensable, and that the whole organization, not the individual, is responsible for acclamation or criticism. Even when one is waiting for the others to finish their parts, one plays, as it were, without sound."

Sunday

It's a 10-minute walk from the apartment to a grocery store. Many apartment tenants go to the store on foot on Sunday morning; they don't talk to each other. Maybe they all like to walk individually or to possess loneliness. An old lady carrying a grocery bag in her arms creates a sense of compassion. Fortunately, it is a downhill from the store to the apartment.

Autumn here is beautiful against the high blue sky. Washington's autumn is as beautiful as its cherry blossom spring. Autumn in the old town is more beautiful, with fall leaves of many colors.

I wrote a poem:

Autumn Vocabularies

Empty beach and footsteps on the sand
Squirrel in the crimson leaves
My neighbor's cold, their underwear and coat

Spinoza's glasses (melancholy falling)
And his long hairs in the wind
Color of the world has been changed
Oh, the red apple, crimson—
The chamber music from inside
My maid dusted the lamp
And the full moon rises on my little villa near the sea.

My essay was sent to my family in Mississippi and my parents in Seoul, Korea. My parents were very happy and proud of my essay. That was my last and little gift to my father who loved poetry and literature, and thought the poet as the bright star in the night sky. He passed away in June 1982.

CHAPTER 18

Death of Father

One June evening in 1982, I received a call from my mother. She told me, "Your Father passed away. I plan for the funeral to be in five days. Until you come, I will keep his body at home." It was a shock to me. My father never went to see the doctor in his life. He was a strong man. His father and grandparents lived very long lives. I did not expect my father die suddenly from a heart attack at 66. Then, I remembered, I did not yet have a U.S. passport, even though I became a naturalized citizen in 1977. I also had a fear to return to the home country because of my anti-Korean government activities in the United States. My office allowed me my sad ten-day trip to Korea. I made a passport in a special express way. I also had a Pentagon paper in my pocket which made it clear that the Office of the Secretary of Defense needed me in a couple of weeks. As long as I was working in the Pentagon, no one in Korea would arrest or jail me for my political activities.

Upon arrival my mother, two sisters, and closer relatives greeted me with tears. My presence at the funeral ceremony was a comfort to my mother and two sisters. My younger brother came from his diplomatic post in Brussels. My sister and her husband in his diplomatic mission in Cameroon could not come to the funeral ceremony.

After I returned from such a sad home-coming trip, I wrote an essay in the *Korea Times*. I reprint it here.

Death of Father

Chased by time, chasing time, grasping it, and letting it go, 15 years have passed since I left Korea. During these years, I lost my grandparents, and most recently my father. I never knew the meaning of death until I lost my father. I knew it was sorrow. But the death of a father is more than sorrow.

For the first time, I found myself an orphan, a lonely man in the wilderness. In the darkness, I rediscovered the value of the letters my father sent to me for these long years saying that "there are always green hills wherever you go," "treat your American friends courteously," "Now, you are forty. I am sure that you have the wisdom to manage your life." "Don't just look at the world! See it!"

I look at myself. I see myself. Sorrow turns into pain. Life is tragic so long as it ends with death. But life is more than tragic when I hear the death of my father thousands of miles away.

Life is short and time is a flowing stream. My father died suddenly from a heart attack, while he was sleeping. My only visit to Korea was for four weeks, eight years before. He tried to hide his tears when I arrived in Seoul after seven years of foreign life. He hated tears in a man's eyes. He was older, but was still healthy.

Every night during my four week visit he was waiting for me at the main gate of Changdok Girls' High School, which is 400 meters from our house. We walked together to our house 400 meters almost every night. He showed his loving care of me in that way. His waiting on the street also prevented me from drinking too much with dear friends who greeted my homecoming after a long absence from the country. He was still a Spartan father.

Why didn't I know life could be so suddenly ended?

Why didn't I know the loss of my father could be the most tragic?

Why didn't I visit Korea once more, twice more......?

Tears turned into crying and weeping when the casket was covered with shovelings of dirt. The casket soon disappeared. He was gone, and a grave was created.

The death of a father is beyond anyone's sorrowful expression. But death has many different meanings to the survivors. Life is one hundred and eight agonies to the Buddhists, and sin to the Christians. Death is and may be a blessing to them. But such a blessing is the survivors' wish. We wish the dead no more sorrow, pain, agony, or tragedy in the heavenly world.

My mother decided the funeral would be held when her two sons returned from foreign countries. My dead father was separated from us by a folding screen for five days and nights. The candle flickers about when life breathes. The burner needed incense to be burned five days and nights.

*Five days and nights, friends of the dead and the survivors mourned, too.
The friends joined the long funeral trip from our house at Kahoe-dong,
Seoul to our mountain at Yongdang-li, Simchon-myon, Youngdong
County, North Choongchung Province. It is very true that Koreans are
the warmest people in the world. They are the kindest people to those
in sorrow.*

*George Siebert, my American friend, tried to persuade me not to go at
the last moment, at the National Airport in Washington, D.C.: "Yearn, you
better think about it. Your father does not know whether you are coming. He
is dead. That is a fact. Think it over! I don't think you reason." He was
concerned about my safe return due to my political writings against the
authoritarian Korean government.*

*My reasoning was different from his. I did not have a choice. I had to
go home for my last homage to my late father, and to share the pain of my
mother and younger sisters.*

*Birds and the fresh green in the home mountains were no different
from those of my last visit eight years ago. The sky was blue. The June field
was busy with farmers' labor. The countryside was not different from that of
the past: The same railroad station, the Kum River, four kilometers of narrow
unpaved road from the Simchon Train Station to our country house, the
empty house for two generations.*

*My father now dwells in the mountains where his parents and
grandparents dwell. Carrying clouds overhead, hugging wind around,
listening to birds and deer, he strolls in the mist. Stepping on the stars
above, he falls asleep, pillowed on the crescent moon.*

*The survivors are in the town. We returned to town. My brother
returned to Brussels and I returned to Washington, D.C.*

I still ask the same question: "Why should I return?"

My best, but not really best, answer is: "My fate."

The wind blows aimlessly.

Distance separates me from Korea. That is all.

*But I have to look at the distance I have to go from this point on.
That is what life is like.*

CHAPTER 19

Defense and the Environment

In 1983, as I was winding up my two-year sojourn at the Pentagon, I was contacted by the editor of *Defense* magazine to write an article on the subject of defense and the environment. The magazine was a publication of the Department of Defense providing official and professional information to commanders and key personnel on matters related to Defense policies, programs, and interests, and to create better understanding and teamwork within the Department of Defense.

Not many people inside and outside the Department of Defense knew much about the existence of the Department's environmental management. So I accepted the invitation.

I produced the article in a week. Then, the editor responded: "This is the article I have been looking for the past two years." Environmental engineers in my office knew much about the subject, but they did not know how to write to meet an editor's expectations for a general public readership. They were very good technical writers, but they did not communicate splendidly with the people outside their field. I was proud of my contribution to *Defense Magazine*, which presented the views on the environment and public policy I had developed as a teacher, and then put into practice in the Pentagon. It might even have been the first article bridging the Department of Defense and the Environment, the two worlds seemingly far apart.

Balancing Environment and the Nation's Defense

Defense, October 1983

The Department of Defense's primary mission is to defend the nation. To many Americans, DOD is symbolized by people in military uniforms, fighters and bombers, aircraft carriers and submarines, tanks and missiles. But the Department of Defense is much more; it is a human organization concerned with the welfare of all the people and the environment they live in. It would make little sense for DOD to be building the defenses of the nation if in doing so it was threatening the health of our environment. To ensure that does not happen, the Department of Defense has a vigorous environmental protection program which has at its center compliance with all federal environmental laws such as the Clean Air Act and the Clean Water Act, the environmental laws of the 50 states, and more than 3,000 local laws and regulations. The importance of this compliance is underscored by DOD's responsibility for protecting the working and living environment for over 4.5 million military personnel and their families, one million civilian workers, and the environment of the land and water it controls.

It follows that the protection extended to DOD personnel, installations, facilities, and equipment from environmental hazards also protects all citizens because environmental hazards such as air and groundwater contamination are not stopped by the boundary lines between DOD installations and neighboring communities.

The National Environmental Policy Act (NEPA) of 1969 was the landmark legislation that "set the Nation on a new course of environmental management." NEPA declared a national policy "fulfilling the responsibility of each generation as trustee of the environment for succeeding generations," and DOD committed itself to supporting it. NEPA addresses federal activities, large and small, and mandates that relevant environmental factors are to be considered at every level of decision-making. When a major action is contemplated, if there is a significant environmental impact, an environmental impact statement (EIS) will be prepared and made available to the President, the Council on Environmental Quality, and the public.

But by the mid-1970s, the environmental review process, which had the best of intentions, was in itself causing problems. It had become increasingly cumbersome. The required statements had become so lengthy and detailed that important issues were often obscured.

New regulations designed to streamline the environmental review process by reducing delays and paperwork and to ensure agency decisions that reflected consideration of all significant environmental issues became effective for most federal agencies in July 1979. These brought the public into the NEPA process at an early stage through a process called "scoping." Scoping allowed interested individuals and communities to participate in identifying issues to be covered by an EIS. The new regulations also directed agencies to limit an EIS to 150 pages and to write it in plain language with the technical information referenced.

So far, DOD has prepared 158 EISs addressing diversified actions such as joint readiness exercises, disposal of toxic and hazardous chemicals, research and development activities, base closures and realignments, construction projects, real estate acquisition, and the removal of animals from our installations. These statements have cost in excess of $50 million, ranging from about $10,000 for a comparatively minor action to over $30 million to date for the MX missile system.

The new regulations have been very helpful to DOD. They have given local community planners and officials an early understanding of how federal projects might affect their communities, as indicated by a county spokesman in Georgia who praised their usefulness in the Navy's Kings Bay submarine base project.

DOD's activities are frequently challenged in court not just by those with environmental concerns but by those opposed to defense policy who see environmental laws as a means to achieve their ends. In *Weinberger v. Catholic Action of Hawaii/Peace Education Project*, the Navy prepared an environmental impact assessment for the construction on the island of Oahu of a facility capable of storing nuclear weapons. The Navy concluded that the project would have no significant impact and that an EIS was unnecessary. The plaintiffs argued that the assessment did not consider the possibility of a nuclear accident if nuclear weapons were stored in the facility and that an EIS should be prepared. The Atomic Energy Act and the directives that implement it prohibit disclosure of information relating to the presence of nuclear weapons at military installations because of national security considerations. The Navy argued that preparation and circulation of an EIS examining the potential impacts of such storage or accidents would disclose classified information.

Although the United States District Court for Hawaii held that the Navy had complied with NEPA "to the fullest extent possible," the Ninth Circuit Court of Appeals disagreed and reversed the lower court's decision. It concluded that an EIS could be written in a way to assess the project without impinging on the problems of national security by analyzing the potential impact of hypothetical storage of nuclear weapons at the facility. The United States Supreme Court, in a unanimous decision, found in favor of the Navy and reversed the appeals court decision. What has emerged from this and other court cases is that the DOD and the military services are not exempt from complying with NEPA because there are classified aspects to the proposed action or because it falls under the broad heading of national security. The latter was demonstrated in the mid-70s with the Air Force's failure to comply with NEPA prior to attempting to move its Communications Service from Richards-Gebaur AFB, Missouri, to Scott AFB, Illinois, which produced several years of litigation.

As the proponent of an action, we must demonstrate that we have taken a hard look at the environmental consequences flowing from what we want to do and that we have considered reasonable alternative courses of action with objective good faith to permit our decision-makers to fully consider and balance the environmental factors involved and the national security interest.

Contrary to popular belief, environmental impact statements do not necessarily work against DOD interests. In 1982, the Federal Aviation Administration (FAA) filed its final EIS for the proposed Palmdale International Airport which would serve the Los Angeles area. After reviewing the statement, DOD pointed out that the FAA had failed to address adequately air space conflicts with DOD operations at the Air Force Flight Test Center at Edwards AFB, Air Force Plant 42, the Naval Weapons Center at China Lake, and Fort Irwin. Meetings to resolve these conflicts are being held.

Major military installations are similar to medium-sized cities and like those cities must deal with the complex environmental problems that exist in any advanced, industrialized society. Some DOD industrial operations which are of particular environmental concern include ammunition plants which manufacture and demilitarize munitions of all types, shipyards, depots, and aircraft and automotive maintenance facilities which generate used oil, spent solvents, cleaners, and electroplating wastes. Many of these wastes are toxic or hazardous materials, and some are suspected cancer-causing carcinogens.

To successfully manage DOD's environmental program for such diverse and complex activities and substances requires a substantial budget, as well as expertise. DOD's pollution abatement authority has grown substantially from its $291 million in Fiscal year 1973. In the 11 years since FY 1973, military construction authority has totaled $1.4 billion.

Such a substantial investment has made DOD a standard-bearer for others to follow in achieving and maintaining a cleaner environment.

DOD, just as the American public, is very concerned with the handling, storage, and disposal of radioactive, toxic, and hazardous materials and their byproducts and waste. Defense-generated high-level radioactive wastes are handled and disposed of by the Department of Energy, but the low-level radioactive wastes are a different matter. They are disposed of at commercial sites or facilities for the latter category of radioactive wastes. Because of the concerns and fears people have about radioactive wastes, states are now forming regional compacts to manage these wastes. In these emerging compacts, which are supposed to go into effect in about three years, there is a sense of fear focused on the acceptance of DOD low-level wastes. Unfortunately, an interruption in the disposal of DOD low-level wastes, most of which are depleted uranium and depleted uranium-contaminated materials, can cause problems affecting the nation's security. This almost happened in 1979 when the Barnwell, South Carolina, commercial site began to decrease the volume of wastes it would accept and two other commercial sites at Beatty, Nevada, and Richland, Washington, were closed periodically. If DOD's temporary waste storage capacities, which were severely strained, had been exceeded, critical defense production lines that generate these wastes would have been stopped.

DOD's prime environmental objective is proper cradle-to-grave management of all hazardous wastes, not just the radioactive varieties. What many people fail to grasp is that disposal practices, such as burial, which were accepted throughout America by municipalities, corporations, and the government a generation or more ago are causing environmental problems today. Ignorance, and in some cases, carelessness, then has come back to create difficulties today. That does not mean that these problems should be put aside; they are real and pressing, and they need to be solved if possible. But we know more today, and DOD is committed through a thorough, expensive, but necessary process involving proper identification, handling, storage, treatment, shipment, and disposal, to the proper management of hazardous wastes.

This requires continuous manifest accountability of the wastes as well as proper Environmental Protection Agency certification of generators, storage sites, transporters, and disposal facilities. The commanders of DOD installations are responsible for ensuring that the necessary operating permits, certifications, and manifest systems are acquired and properly maintained. DOD generated an estimated 92,000 tons of hazardous wastes in 1981, a very small percentage of the estimated 57 million tons of waste the nation as a whole produced that year. Despite the small percentage of the national output involved, it was recognized that these dangerous wastes require a central point for proper management within DOD.

The Defense Logistics Agency (DLA) has the broad charter of being DOD's single manager for the disposal of most hazardous wastes generated by military activities. Within DLA, this job was focused in the Defense Property Disposal Service, headquartered in Battle Creek, Michigan. The Defense Property Disposal Service in addition to ensuring that toxic and hazardous wastes are disposed of in accordance with federal, state, and local laws and regulations also evaluates the salvage and resale possibilities for these materials. An excellent example of these efforts was the Army's sale of 368 tons of the World War I chemical agent, phosgene. A firm in New York bought the chemical for use in urethane plastic manufacturing. Collection, storage, and disposal of toxic and hazardous wastes is done through 142 Defense Property Disposal Service offices collocated with military installations throughout the world and 74 off-installation branches which contract disposal actions to commercial firms. Through these offices, DLA has disposed of over 150,000 gallons of polychlorinated biphenyls (PCB), the highly toxic material used primarily as a transformer coolant, at EPA-approved facilities. Similarly, 240,000 gallons, 210,000 pounds of powder, and 62,000 aerosol cans of DDT have been collected. All but the liquid has been destroyed, and it will be disposed of on an oceangoing incinerator ship.

DOD's installation restoration program, which concentrates on past operations, began in 1975. The program was initiated out of our concern for environmental quality and the public's health and welfare; not because of any legislative mandate. In this program, the Army, Navy, Air Force, and Defense Logistics Agency are conducting a careful review of past hazardous material disposal sites on DOD facilities to identify, evaluate, and control as necessary any potential dangers to people or the environment. The same careful review procedures are being applied to land and facilities excess to the DOD mission which will pass to non-DOD ownership. The military departments and DLA have been required by DOD to establish and operate the installation restoration program, to complete record searches (the first phase of the review) at every installation listed on service priority lists by the end of FY 1985, and to develop and maintain a priority list of contaminated installations and facilities requiring remedial action.

Probably the most publicized past environmental contamination involving DOD is the Rocky Mountain Arsenal near Denver. The arsenal was established in 1942 to produce toxic chemicals and incendiary munitions. Beginning in 1946, portions of the arsenal were leased to private industry for chemical manufacturing operations. Shell Chemical Company has been the major lessee since 1952. It has manufactured various pesticides and herbicides at the arsenal. In 1974, two chemical byproducts of nerve agent and pesticide manufacturing were detected in surface and ground waters. This led the State of Colorado to issue cease and desist orders to the Army and Shell in 1975. Army studies confirmed the groundwater was contaminated and migrating off the installation. The Army has sought to first stop contamination migration beyond the arsenal boundaries, and second, to identify and control sources of contamination. To date, it has spent $45 million for studies and corrective projects at the arsenal. It is believed that the off-post migration of contaminants will finally be halted by next year.

Another well-publicized incident was when the Air Force discovered groundwater contamination problems at Wurtsmith AFB, Michigan, in 1977. Trichloroethylene (TCE), an industrial degreasing solvent and suspected carcinogen, had found its way into the groundwater from a leaking underground tank. While this was being investigated, three other unrelated contamination problems were found. The TCE contamination eventually made one off-base and several on-base wells un-potable. The Air Force emptied the leaking tank and began to pump groundwater to prevent the spread of contamination. Eventually, the Air Force spent over $1.8 million to develop and construct a system for stripping TCE from the water at Wurtsmith.

The Department of Defense has great expertise and probably more experience than anyone in the identification, characterization, and control of environmental contaminants. We believe strongly in the systematic approach we have taken and are convinced that positive action to protect the public can result from just such a dedicated systematic program. DOD set its Superfund Program much earlier than the US Congress enacted the

Superfund Law. To date, DOD's environmental achievements have been significant. But the future will require additional, substantial efforts. Secretary of Defense Caspar Weinberger made DOD's commitment to this cause quite clear last fall when he said:

"Environmental protection has become a way of life for us in the Defense Department. We have worked hard to ensure that managers of all our facilities, ships, and installations continuously maintain an awareness of the environmental laws and regulations which govern them. We have aggressively sought solutions to pollution problems which were created in the past. Environmental consideration is a key element in DOD's planning for future actions. We are proud of our environmental achievements, and we maintain a continuing commitment to environmental protection throughout DOD."

* * * * *

The front page article of the *Washington Post* on June 30, 2008, *Pentagon Fights EPA On Pollution Cleanup,* and the follow-up article on July 1, *Senators Fault Pentagon On Bases' Toxic Cleanup,* both by Lyndsey Layton, may be a serious charge against the Pentagon for its non-compliance with the nation's environmental laws and regulations, including Maryland's. The Pentagon is supposed to comply with all laws and regulations. That is why I cannot understand the Pentagon's intent or non-compliance. The articles did not explain or disclose the Pentagon's reason or excuses.

The Pentagon had initiated what is called the Installation Restoration (IR) Program long before the US Congress passed the "Superfund" law in order to clean up its chemical waste dump sites at the Rocky Mountain Arsenal in Colorado and other states. When I was working for the Pentagon as an assistant for environmental quality two decades ago, I was proud of the IR program, which was a promising start.

The problem then, and I presume now, is that the IR program's limited resources prevented the clean-up operation of the sites. We instead began to launch a containment policy, which was much less expensive. We tried to control the sites at least in order not to contaminate the ground water and soil. I am sure the situation today is not very different from the 1980s. Nevertheless, the Pentagon paid great attention to the imminent dangers to public health. It should protect public health always.

The article was somewhat mistaken when it stated that the Pentagon's non-compliance was unprecedented. During my time, the Pentagon did not agree with the EPA on several issues. Then, the OMB was the final mediator or arbitrator in inter-departmental disputes. I am quite sure that intergovernmental disputes or conflicts are still prevailing, and the OMB's role is ever present. The Federal-State conflicts have been serious since the days of the Founding Fathers. McCulloch v. Maryland, (1819) was the first landmark case. From that ground alone, the State of Maryland can sue the Pentagon, and win the case with the support of the environmental groups, even if the legal process stretches over a long period. Political solutions are always desirable. The Senators' letter of July 1 (Sen. Robert Menendez (N.J.), Sens. Frank Lautenberg (N.J.), Barbara A. Mikulski (Md.), Benjamin L. Cardin (Md.), Bill Nelson (Fla.), and Sen. Barbara Boxer (Calif.)) to the Secretary of Defense would bring a new response from the Pentagon.

Very obviously, the Pentagon should comply with Maryland's environmental laws and regulations. Military installations are first of all human organizations, with human vulnerabilities. For that reason alone they must also be environmental organizations. What good is the defense of a polluted, unhealthy nation?

CHAPTER 20

Nuclear (Radioactive) Waste Management

During my two-year stint at the Pentagon, I dealt with low-level waste within the framework of the Radioactive Waste Policy Act of 1980. Among other things, this meant that not much got done during my two years at the Pentagon. I met many people in the Council of State Governments, engineering inter-state compacts and lobbying congressional staff. I attended congressional committee hearings. But the overall policy barely budged. After I left the Pentagon, the law has been amended, but very little has been done. This is an example of the often pathetic politicking and maneuvering that goes on between and among the country's 50 states. Nuclear waste management is a mission impossible.

There have been some dramatic changes in the United States and the world in the past twenty-five years. The Department of Defense now has an assistant secretary for environmental affairs, and the nation's environmental programs have been upgraded. But nothing has been done to implement the law on radioactive waste. The spirit of inter-state compacts that the law advocated has been missing. Waste reduction technology has been improved as a byproduct of the law, but that's about it.

Nuclear waste has been generated in the United States ever since the Manhattan Project in 1943. Since this moment ushered the world into the Nuclear Age, the use of nuclear energy, and products thereof, as well as the reliance upon nuclear arms, have been increasingly common and prolific. However, the U.S. and other nuclear nations have not yet found satisfactory ways to dispose of nuclear waste. Past governmental and scientific efforts to manage radioactive waste have not always been politically and technically adequate. The basic human fear of radioactivity still prevails. No one wants the waste, usually for NIMBY reasons — Not in My Backyard. The animosity toward radioactive waste is much more intense than it is toward chemical waste, solid waste, or even a prison in one's backyard.

By the late 1980s, the 96th Congress had reached some consensus on comprehensive legislation to deal with high-level waste, low-level waste, so-called "transuranic" waste, and spent fuel. This legislation incorporated many of the principal recommendations of two leading groups in this area, the Interagency Review Group and State Planning Council on Radioactive Waste Management. However, in the last week of the session, an impasse arose over two issues: (1) the application of the policy on defense high-level waste and transuranic waste, and (2) the role of the Federal government in the storage of commercial spent fuel. On the last day of the session, Congress cut out those provisions of the omnibus bill dealing with commercial low-level waste and passed the 1980 Low-Level Radioactive Waste Policy Act.

Civilian nuclear power reactors and the production of nuclear weapons produce high-level and low-level radioactive wastes. High-level waste is used reactor fuel; low-level waste is everything else from discarded protective clothing to contaminated equipment. Low-level waste might emit any combination of alpha, beta, or gamma radiation, produced by radioisotopes with very short or very long half-lives. It is much less radioactive than high-level waste. Low-level radioactive waste in the United States and Japan, as well as in several European nations, has typically been buried in shallow landfills. No nation has yet devised a satisfactory permanent disposal site for high-level waste, although Norway and the United States have designated potential sites.

The United States: A Crisis in the Future?

Senator John Kerry, campaigning in the state of Nevada in 2004, made a very serious pledge not to use Yucca Mountain as the nation's high-level nuclear waste disposal site. I wish he had not made this pledge. It set back U.S. waste disposal efforts measurably.

For all his other shortcomings, I credit President George W. Bush with a courageous decision on this subject when he designated Yucca Mountain as a permanent nuclear waste disposal site. His decision was extremely unpopular in Nevada. But the U.S. Congress endorsed it. It had taken more than 20 years to get here. The U.S. Department of Energy has been searching for the best available site in the nation since the passage of the Nuclear Waste Policy Act in 1982. The Nuclear Regulatory Commission's licensing process is the project's next hurdle. Sen. Kerry cannot reverse the progress made so far.

The oft-heard alternative, proposed back then also by Sen. Kerry, is an international consortium to dispose nuclear waste. This has been discussed and studied by a panel of National Research Council scientists and engineers, who conclude that the United States could engage Russia and China to propose disposal sites in Central Asia and the Gobi Desert. That may be possible in the distant future. But for now the transportation would simply be far too costly.

If the United States rejects the Yucca Mountain site on the grounds of geological safety, I don't think any site can be considered safe in this world. If that is the case, then all nations should close down their nuclear power plants and stop nuclear weapons production. We can stop nuclear weapons production, but can we close down the nuclear power plants? Maybe the United States could, relying as it does on nuclear power for only 20 percent of its electricity (even then it would be a serious blow in this era of high energy prices). But South Korea, my home country, generates 50 percent of its electricity from nuclear power. China, India, Japan, and the Southeast Asian nations are expanding their nuclear power programs to supply their future energy needs. It is not very realistic.

Based upon the voluminous findings of waste research over the last quarter century, the U.S. Department of Energy chose the Nevada site as the "least bad" of all the options. There is probably no single ideal site, but it is fair to say that Yucca Mountain is one of the best available. Environmentalists seeking a no-risk society need a reality check. Of course, some American politicians and intellectuals speak about it anyway. U.S. scientists and engineers have examined and reexamined the research findings, and made a positive response. I trust their work.

The Democratic Party has a favorable environmental record as a political party, but giving up the Yucca Mountain site is environmentally unethical. The Clinton administration postponed the decision to finalize the Nevada site for political reasons. The U.S. has generated nuclear waste since the Manhattan Project in the 1940s. Avoiding responsibility may be good politics, but it's unpresidential and unwise. President Bill Clinton could also have ratified the Kyoto Protocol, or could (at least) have made an attempt to ratify it. He did not. The Bush administration made a decision against the Protocol, a decision that has been harshly criticized by the international community. President Clinton was also responsible for the failure of California's search for a disposal site for low-level waste on federal land in California. I wonder whether the Clinton administration deserved its high evaluation in the field of environmental policy and management.

I wish Sen. Kerry would at least have acknowledged reality by proposing a new moratorium on nuclear power plants and nuclear weapons production, since this is what his proposal ultimately means. He didn't of course. He could even have proposed a retrievable disposal facility in Nevada, assuming that future science can find and invent safer disposal sites and methods. He did not say that either. He just said, No Yucca Mountain disposal on my watch! This is political, no more and no less. It turns the world back to 1982.

Even the U.S. nuclear energy industry is having difficulty finding low-level waste disposal sites. The two disposal sites in South Carolina and Washington that existed prior to the 1980 Low-Level Radioactive Waste Policy Act had been taking waste from all 50 states. The 1980 act proposed that low-level waste disposal should be the responsibility of state or interstate compacts, but as of yet no new site has been opened. This is a very serious problem for the United States. It has set a bad example to the outside world. Finding nuclear waste disposal sites must be the most difficult task in American politics.

* * * * *

The law governing low-level radioactive waste is a case study in the dilemmas of federalism. Here's how. The LLW Policy Act established a federal policy that a state is responsible for providing waste disposal capacity for low-level radioactive waste generated within its borders. The act provided that:

(1) Each state is responsible for providing for the availability of capacity either within or outside the state for the disposal of commercial low-level radioactive waste generation within its borders.

(2) LLW can be most safely and efficiently managed on a regional basis.

(3) States may enter into compacts that may restrict the use of regional disposal facilities to LLW generated within the region.

Regionalization by interstate compact has thus been the primary permissible means for states to assume the responsibilities outlined in the act. By January 1, 1986, the states or the interstate compacts were supposed to begin to operate disposal facilities.

Nothing really happened. No new disposal facilities have been established even as of 2004. In 1986, six regional compacts were formed: the Northwest Compact (Washington, Oregon, Utah, Idaho, Arkansas, Hawaii); the Southeast Compact (South Carolina, Georgia, Alabama, Mississippi, Florida, North Carolina, Tennessee, Virginia); Rocky Mountain Compact. (Nebraska, Wyoming, Colorado, Arizona, New Mexico); the Midwest Compact (Illinois, Indiana, Ohio, Michigan, Wisconsin, Minnesota, Iowa, South Dakota, Nebraska, Kentucky); the Northeast Compact (New York, Pennsylvania, Maryland, Delaware, Massachusetts, Connecticut, Rhode Island, Vermont, New Hampshire, Maine), and the Central Compact (Kansas, Oklahoma, Arkansas, Louisiana). Texas, California, West Virginia, and North Dakota were unaffiliated.

Three regions had existing disposal facilities: Northwest at Hanford, WA; Southeast at Barnwell, SC; and Rocky Mountain at Betty which was closed in early 1990s. The interstate compacts seemed promising at first but simply did not move forward. No state wants nuclear dumps within its borders. No state wants to host new dumps within its borders or even in the region. That has been the most serious problem. Each state harbored the wishful expectation that a neighboring state would create an initial disposal site. Naturally, regional compacts could not be successful on so much wishful thinking and expectations.

The Barnwell dump had been operating to receive the nation's waste, but starting in 2008 it began banning all waste coming from outside the Atlantic regional compact states. So, many states cannot send and dispose their radioactive waste to Barnwell. This is a crisis, or at least the beginning of one. I don't understand the American mentality here.

In 2009 I asked Nancy Zacha about it. As editor of *Radwaste Solutions*, a publication of the American Nuclear Society, she follows this subject closely. As she emailed me, "Since Barnwell is closed to all waste generators except Atlantic Compact state generators on June 30, waste generators in other states are storing their waste, or sending it to waste processors to volume-reduce it (and then storing the smaller volume of waste)."

"Two companies (Studsvik and Waste Control Specialists) are offering a service whereby Studsvik treats the waste and volume reduces it, and Waste Control Specialists stores the waste until a new storage facility open to all waste generators is available (even though that could be years from now). Hospitals, universities, industrial, and research facilities might be the ones who will most likely take advantage of this service, because they typically do not have available space for storing nuclear waste. Nuclear power plants, on the other hand, know how to handle waste, and usually have room to store it."

"It's too early to tell if there is a crisis or not. I CERTAINLY think there is a crisis, but the Nuclear Regulatory Commission does not think so (there is no health and safety crisis, and that is all they are worried about). When the currently operating nuclear power plants start decommissioning and there are suddenly millions of pounds of waste to be disposed of, THEN there really will be a crisis. But with most of the nuclear power plants in the U.S. going for license renewals, that means they will not begin decommissioning for at least another 20 or so years, at the earliest. Some plants are talking about renewing licenses again and again, until a plant has operated up to 100 years, but that's way into the future."

* * * * *

It is stunning. Ever since legislation was passed in 1980 to govern low-level radioactive waste, nothing has been done except for waste

reduction. This is such irresponsible behavior on the part of the states! There has been simply no inter-state cooperation or decency. Class-A waste, which comprises 95 percent of low-level waste, will be shipped to the Envirocare of Utah. But Class B and C will be stored temporarily at nuclear power plants, hospitals and university labs. Or low-level radioactive waste will be temporarily stored at the two private companies forever. Class B and C, more dangerous waste, will be classified into A in the future, so that all low-level radioactive waste will be shipped to the Envirocare of Utah.

The Yucca Mountain site for high-level waste disposal may not even be open in the year 2020 or later, despite the fact that Congress passed the Nuclear Waste Policy Act way back in 1982.

I don't understand the politics of radioactive waste management in this country at all. It is a kind of humpty-dumpty mentality.

The US Ecology site in Richland, Washington has been receiving waste from the 11 states of the Northwest and Rocky Mountain Compacts. Texas has a new law in force that provides Class A/B/C disposal capacity for members of the Texas Compact (Texas and Vermont). The Envirocare of Utah site accepts Class A waste at what are considered reasonably disposal fees and so receives the bulk of the nation's Class A waste. Class A waste require minimum precautions for disposal. Class B waste must meet minimum requirements. Class C waste should be guarded from a future "inadvertent intruder."

If the present state continues, 34 states will not have any place to dispose for B/C waste.

After 25 years, no new state or compact disposal facility has opened. Or been licensed. Or been developed. Or even been designated. Nancy Zacha reviewed the 1980 act. The main problem is lawsuits. "In fact, it appears that the only beneficiaries of the act today are lawyers, who are doing a thriving business. There are lawsuits pending against North Carolina (a reluctant host state being sued by its compact), Nebraska (another reluctant host state whose governor was found to have actively tried to scuttle licensing activities), and California (being sued by US Ecology for recovery of the $160 million the company spent in developing the California site). In addition, there is a countersuit by Nebraska against the compact. As with many lawsuits, these have been ongoing for several years and probably still have several more years to run," she wrote.

Steven Kraft, director of waste management of the Nuclear Energy Institute agreed with her view in his meeting with me, when I visited NEI on September 3, 2004.

So, what is a waste generator to do? Is there a path forward?

For many nuclear power plants, the answer lies in reducing or eliminating the generation of B/C waste. Clint Miller, a waste engineer at Pacific Gas and Electric, reported an effort at several plant alliances under the Strategic Teaming and Resources Sharing (STARS), all located west of the Mississippi River. Primarily, such efforts involve changing out resin beds more frequently and changing packaging methods. Utilities are also looking at extended waste storage capacity and perhaps more effective waste treatment methods.

There is also the very slight chance that the state of South Carolina will change its mind and keep the Barnwell facility open. South Carolina, like almost all states these days, is looking at budget shortfalls. Keeping Barnwell open, and increasing B/C disposal fees, might be a way to generate some needed income. At this time, there is no indication that the state is leaning in this direction, but it closed Barnwell once before and reopened it, so an optimist can always hope for history to repeat itself.

Envirocare of Utah might decide to pursue the B/C license in the future. This will, in part, depend on the climate in the state legislature and governorship. Utah is replacing its governor this year (former Governor Mike Leavitt was recently appointed to head the US Environmental Protection Agency). An improved political climate and a new governor following the November elections who is sympathetic to nuclear power/radioactive waste management would be needed to make it possible.

* * * * *

I firmly believe that all states should be responsible for managing their own radioactive waste within their own borders, or ideally be ready to host the regional waste. The stuff has to go somewhere.

I wrote a commentary on regional compacting in *Pollution Engineering* in 1983:

"Despite its low-level, this waste generates fear. No one wants radioactive waste in his or her backyard. Fear is due to radioactivity and our imperfect control of it. Our state of knowledge should be attributed as a major cause of the fear. Even today, monitoring is an imprecise science: different types of radiations causing varying effects to various parts of the body are registered differently by detection devices. Furthermore, such factors as radiation pathways and mobility and mechanisms whereby radioactivity might concentrate in organisms are not completely understood. Small wonder, then, that reputable estimates of the hazards posed by exposure to low levels of a particular type of radiation may differ by very large factors. There are the basic disagreements that, in part, fuel much of the debate over the radioactive waste problem."

I took to emphasizing the role of fear in these debates. I also emphasized the nuclear scientist's role as an educator to the public. I still like to say the same thing today.

Ironically, the present energy crisis may just be the solution we've been looking for. It could open nuclear power as an alternative, and greatly increase its use. At some point, this forces states to reckon more realistically with their own "Not in My Backyard" resistance.

CHAPTER 21

Life in Washington

My fellowship was over. I spent two great years watching the bureaucracy in action. I could now incorporate these governmental experiences into my teaching and research activities. I could apply concepts such as management by objectives (MBO) and cost-benefit analysis to the real world of public administration. Inside the Department of Defense, the Army, Navy, Air Force and Marine Corps were each asked to report their environmental management practices from an MBO perspective to my office. Their objectives were basically compliances with the environmental laws and regulations, or reduction of violations each year. I comparatively used cost-benefit analyses of clean-up efforts and the contamination costs and benefits of hazardous waste dump sites.

One most unforgettable experience was the least expensive award ceremony ever for the Secretary of Defense Environmental Award and the Secretary of Defense Conservation Award. The cost was $50 for coffee, tea and pastries, but the benefit was much more than that. There was immeasurable joy and happiness for the winning installations. The idea was simple: Recognize and honor the leading performers. The award ceremony may be still going on. It should be. The award offered a great stimulus to all military installations to protect the environment and conserve nature. My two-year governmental experiences offered this kind of very practical value to my teaching and research works in the following years.

Before my fellowship was over, I was offered a teaching job by the University of the District of Columbia College of Business and Public Management downtown. I accepted it without hesitation. I had enjoyed teaching, and decided I would enjoy a return to my old profession more than I would a government job. I was free inside and outside the university. My scholarly articles were suspiciously seen as a product of "company time" by my boss in the Pentagon, who seemed to prefer that I not publish at all.

The University of District of Columbia never developed a winning reputation for itself, even though it had the potential. Part of the problem was the competition. Georgetown University, George Washington University, American University and Catholic University surround UDC and offer stark comparisons. I tried to maintain my reputation as a college professor and researcher. I continuously engaged in research activities and published scholarly papers while teaching public administration courses at the master's degree program. I was the public administration specialist in the department of management. The MPA program was small compared to the MBA program in terms of student enrollment and faculty size. But the management department viewed the difference between business and government organizations as marginal. So the adjective "public" was overwhelmed by the noun "management." I enjoyed courses including Government-Business Relations, which I had never taught before. Environmental policy is a good regulatory area of government-business relations. Deregulation was a fashionable term in the 1980s. Optimum regulation was always sought after. Deregulation was not non-regulation, but was misinterpreted by many conservative politicians. I wrote an article, "Is Big Government an Endangered Species?" published in the *World & I* in May, 1986. I was happy to write such an article against the conservative tide of the Reagan era as a public administration scholar.

The department chairman was Hany Makhlouf, an Egyptian educated at American University. We were good friends who discussed the situations in our home countries during our leisure time, especially lunch hours. He appreciated my role as a colleague who set up high achievement goals as a teacher, a researcher, and a community server.

In the meantime, I continued writing for the public press. I was struck at this time by the deep problems of Washington, D.C. It is our nation's capitol, and yet it was afflicted with such awful social ills. In a *Washington Times* Op-Ed, I decried the state of inner-city Washington, which at that point had reached an awful crescendo of drug-related violence and social pathology. Still today large sections of Washington are the same, although much of the eastern part of Northwest D.C. have revitalized, as has Chinatown, and parts of the waterfront. Back then, the city gave no signs of the coming revitalization. As I put it: "I see the District as a poverty stricken city in the Third World. Very few feel pride in the nation's capital. Most do not care that it has become the murder capital. Northern Virginia and Maryland local governments in the Washington metropolitan area all enjoy the tremendous benefits of being neighbors to the capital, but they don't care about the inner city's problem. If there were no capital in the District, they would be just leisurely towns as in the South and Midwest." With adjustments to reflect the gentrification of a few parts of Washington, these sentences are basically as true today as they were back then.

My wife found a job at an army hospital as a pharmacist. She was happy to resume her old profession, finally. The job came after a long preparation. She first worked as an assistant to the pharmacist (pharmacy technician) for 2,000 hours, and then passed the TOEFL test (required score of 550). Then, she was qualified to take a qualifying exam for foreign pharmacists at Miami, Florida. She flew to Miami to take the test and passed that exam. Then, she was allowed to take the state board of pharmacy exam. She took the State of Maryland's exam, because the State of Virginia did not accept foreign pharmacists. She took the exam with the graduates of University of Maryland School of Pharmacy at Baltimore, Maryland. She passed. Finally, she became an American pharmacist after years of preparation. She could find a job in the State of Maryland or in a federal hospital. So she got a job at an army hospital in Alexandria, Virginia.

Our life in Northern Virginia was happy. Our two children started elementary school and loved it. They joined the community soccer team, swimming team, tennis team and T-Ball teams, and I gave them a ride to the field almost every weekend.

* * * * *

Living in Washington affords a person opportunities to meet the most influential people in U.S.-Korean relations. Two who stand out, whom I met and interviewed at length, are Wendy Gramm, wife of a former senator and previously the highest-ranking Korean-American woman in the U.S. government, and Ezra Vogel, one of the leading academics on East Asian affairs in the United States.

Wendy Gramm

Wendy Gramm has been exposed to much news coverage since she was appointed to the chairmanship of the Commodity Futures Trading Commission from 1988-1993. Born in Hawaii, Gramm identifies herself as a Korean-American, and makes many speeches to the Korean organizations in the Washington area.

I was glad to meet her in her office, and was happy to listen to her speeches. She knows her grandfather's life as a contracted laborer in the Hawaii sugarcane fields. He came in the first wave of immigrants from Korea in 1903, the last days of the Yi dynasty. Later he became a construction worker. His son, Wendy Gramm's father, was an engineer, and later became vice president of the sugarcane company his father once worked as a laborer. Wendy Lee Gramm was born in 1945, educated at Wellesley and received a Ph.D. in economics from Northwestern University. She then became a professor of economics at Texas A & M University, where she met her husband-to-be. When her husband was elected to the U.S. Senate, she moved to Washington, D.C. and worked for the Office of Management and Budget, and the White House.

Her family story of three generations caught President Ronald Reagan's attention, and was extensively used in his speech in the 1988 Asian-Pacific Heritage Week. President Reagan cited her family as a model example of Asian immigrants to the United States, and emphasized their educational achievements, their family-oriented life style, and their diligence and hard work. Certainly Wendy's family deserves the presidential speech.

In a speech to the Korean-American Citizens League some years ago, Gramm asked the first generation of Korean immigrants to remember always why they came here and to remind them why they are here. The United States is the land of opportunity, so she advised them to achieve what they can achieve. But that was not all she said.

I appreciated her advice to the Koreans to transfer the Korean language, preserve Korean culture, and conserve Korean memories to the next generation. She told us about her mother, who was the first Korean from Hawaii to receive U.S. citizenship. When she was asked why she should be a U.S. citizen, she answered: "I came here, live here, and work hard here."

Wendy vividly remembers her mother's statement and praised her mother's "commonsensible, but most powerful statement" to the U.S. Immigration Officer. She was proud of her mother. Mother was proud of being a Korean. I admired this empathy. Third generation Koreans usually lose touch with the ancestral country. Not Wendy.

During my trip to the University of Hawaii, I met Gramm's mother, Angeline, who was kind enough to talk to me one afternoon about her life experience and to give me her cookbook she printed for her children, which included a recipe for Kimchi.

I asked Wendy in her office: "What can you do for Korea?"

She answered: "My support of free trade is my support of Korea." Her answer was very much an economist's.

She confessed to me that she was really touched by many calls and letters from Korean people in Korea, Europe, and the United States.

I am quite sure that many Koreans all over the world are happy to know her, as I am. Gramm is a model Korean to all Korean-Americans, and is inspiring many young Koreans to move upward toward the top of society.

Gramm reminds me of Cathy Song, another third-generation Korean woman from Hawaii. Her "Picture bride" received the 1982 Yale Younger Poets Award. I discussed Cathy Song's poems with Wendy's Mother during my stay in Hawaii. Both are outstanding Korean-Americans of the third generation. I sure hoped that my daughter, part of the second generation, could pick up something from them.

Ezra Vogel on Asia

I met Ezra Vogel at his home near Harvard. He is a professor of international affairs and of sociology at Harvard University. He has been director of the East Asian Research Center and director of the program on U.S.-Japan relations there. Perhaps his most famous book is, *Japan as Number One*. Vogel has visited Korea many times, has many Korean friends, including Kim Dae-jung and Kim Kyung-won, the Harvard-educated former ambassador to the United States (1985-88). I interviewed him for the *Korea Herald* in 1988, and his answers are still interesting today.

Q: What do you expect from Korea-China relations?

A: Slow but positive change. China cannot move quickly. China is a Communist nation, and is a nation friendly to North Korea.

Q: How do you evaluate China's modernization efforts?

A: Chinese modernization or development is very uneven. The pace of development is all different. Each region is quite autonomous. I will give you examples: Northeast region, Manchuria, is the Korean region. Koreans there are more well-educated than any other ethnic groups in China. Shanghai is a very bureaucratic city. But the area 50 to 100 miles west of Shanghai along the river is rapidly developing. Guangdong, or Canton, is rapidly developing because Hong Kong businessmen have invested a lot of money there. It is the region growing fast.

Q: Why is Shanghai not?

A: It is a bureaucratically controlled city. It lost flexibility. Larger bureaucracy is complex which often loses innovative ideas and thoughts. Smaller communities are more innovative, less bureaucratic.

Q: Is the big bureaucracy that bad?

A: Yes. Bureaucracy which manages land is rigid. Bureaucracy which manages machinery and equipment is also rigid. When you try to do business with them, you only see difficulties.

Q: What is Korea's gain from China's modernization?

A: Korea's chance is there. China has been trying to diversify its contacts with other nations. Japan has been its main contact. But their relationships have ups and downs. 1972 was up, 1978 was down. 1988 is up. Korea and Taiwan will be alternative sources of supply to China. China admires Korea's development. China needs Korea's industrial goods — tools and machinery. Koreans in Manchuria will play an important intermediary role for Korea and China. They are neutral to two Koreas. Koreans should develop contacts with China's different provinces. There cannot be one China policy in trade and investment, because every province has different sets of policies and different economic needs.

Q: Is Korea a competitor to Japan?

A: Yes, it is. But they have common interest in business. Koreans are the best people to understand the Japanese people.

Q: How do you see Korea-Japan relations outside business?

A: Mutually antagonistic.

Q: Why 'mutually'? Only Koreans were hurt by the Japanese colonial rule.

A: Antagonistic feelings between Korea and Japan had been there long before the Japanese colonial rule. Even before Hideoyoshi's invasion of Korea, Korea had been scared of the Japanese people. Koreans were forced to come to Japan as slaves. Those who came to Japan as laborers during the Japanese rule over Korea remained in Japan after the Liberation of 1945. But they and their children's upward social mobility is still very limited. Some criminals are Koreans. But the Japanese people exaggerate that kind of statistics. The Japanese people are very nationalistic. Koreans in Japan are nationalistic. They are not happy.

Q: How do you see four dragons in the year 2000?

A: Korean economy will remain strong. Wage is low. Technology has room for improvement. Taiwan will be strong in high-tech. Hong Kong will be meant by Hong Kong-Guangdong. They are already one. Hong Kong-Guangdong will be like Korea and Taiwan. Singapore's economy is so small that it has limits. They will be very competitive. Probably more goods may be available than people can buy. Their manufacturing capacity will be more efficient. They will be able to produce more goods and services.

Q: How do you predict two Koreas in the year 2000?

A: Positively. North Korea cannot be isolated long. Reforms in China and the USSR will certainly affect North Korea. Opening is inevitable. Pressure is strong. If not, North Korea cannot keep up with other nations. Unification is unrealistic. But two Koreas will be like Taiwan and China.

Q: Do you expect protectionism will be less popular or more popular in the United States?

A: I cannot tell. But I can tell you that the United States cannot continue its enormous trade deficit. Japan and Korea should buy more from the United States.

Q: One last question. Your book, *Japan as Number One*, made you famous. The book was criticized by some scholars. Can you respond to that criticism from today's perspective?

A: Yes. Some critics said that my book exaggerated Japanese science and technology. Now, they admit that Japanese science and technology are strong. So there is greater recognition of my book now more than ever before.

From the *Korea Herald*, June 17, 1988.

Our discussion in the summer of 1988 is still interesting in part because Shanghai has turned out to be so different from Vogel's forecast. China-South Korea trade has increased in volume, but an emerging conflict between China and Korea occasionally flares up. One is when China tries to incorporate the Koguryo Kingdom into Chinese history — an insult to Koreans to be sure. Then there are other aspects: North Korea is basically the same closed nation under the dictator. The "rise of Japan" craze of the 1980s and 1990s died down when Japanese growth stagnated. Japanese science and technology is no longer directly comparable to that of the United States, or, at least, it is not viewed as a competitive threat like it once was.

Thoughts on government: Is Big Government an Endangered Species?

Years earlier, I had felt a chill go through me when listening to President Reagan's first inaugural address. Our problems, he said, are not problems government can solve; rather, government is the problem. Indeed, we do have problems for which government has no solution, and some of our problems are indeed caused by government.

But if government itself is the "problem," then, suggests Dwight Waldo, a Syracuse professor emeritus and former editor in chief of *Public Administration Review*, is the problem solved by abolishing government?

I listened to many more Reagan speeches following the inauguration in 1981. Luckily, we still have government, and Reagan is the chief executive of the government, although if Reagan is succeeded by another Reaganite, the government may become an extinct species. Shall we then enact a law for the protection of the government? How about the Endangered Government Act?

The 1973 Endangered Species Act does not cover human institutions. Maybe it should. It covers animals and plants, yet government is surely more precious than snail darters (a species of three-inch, tannish-colored perch), or any other endangered life form currently under the protection of law.

Alfred Marshall, a noted economist, remarked that government is the most precious of human possessions, and that no effort can be too great when spent in enabling government to do its work in the best way. Through most of recorded history, politics and government, not private enterprise or business administration, have been at center stage. I don't know whether or not future times will hand private or business administration primacy over the affairs of the state. But whatever the future holds, the role of government will doubtless be preserved within the structure of society.

We created government out of particular needs and circumstances. The American experiment was inaugurated with the establishment of a federal government two hundred years ago, and the political system that has evolved remains the precious legacy of the Founding Fathers at the Philadelphia Convention.

Early laissez-faire economic policies, which promoted the survival of the fittest, did brutal damage to the economic order. In response to certain abuses (for example, in the railroad industry, which suffered from hasty construction, stock-watering, market manipulation, kickbacks, and other forms of unethical treatment), Congress enacted regulatory legislation to curb some business activities, which in turn resulted in the formation of independent regulatory agencies. The Interstate Commerce Commission, for instance, was created in 1887 in order to protect both consumers and business.

During the New Deal era, the government ultimately intervened because the private sector could not solve the problems. Progress demanded that the government assume the role of arbiter of the goods and scarce resources in the 1930s, and again, to become the promoter of ethics and social justice in the 1960s.

Regulatory, redistributive, and ethical functions made our government big, perhaps too big. Big is always a relative concept.

Those functions, though, were mandated by a collective American will. The government has responded to citizens' desires, and although citizens' desires sometimes may be unrealistic, irrational, and otherworldly they nevertheless reflect certain ideas in the nation at different time periods. Public calls for decent jobs, housing, health care, and other life necessities were behind much congressional legislation.

In a democratic system, politicians transfer or convert the citizens' desires into legislative language. The legislative language should articulate the nation's goals and policies out of the broad-based desires of the citizens. Congress sometimes fails to translate citizens' desires into proper legislative policy, in which case the legislation remains vague and ineffective.

The National Housing Act of 1948, for instance, declared "the realization as soon as feasible of the goal of a decent home and a suitable living environment for every American family." The Federal Water Pollution Control Act of 1972 had as its goals the elimination of discharge of pollutants into navigable waters by 1985 and water quality which allows for the protection and propagation of fish, shellfish, wildlife, and human recreation — to be achieved by July 1, 1983. The Low-Level Radioactive Waste Policy Act of 1980 established January 1, 1986, as the start-up date for operation of new low-level radioactive waste disposal sites. These laws among others demonstrate congressional failures in transforming the citizens' desires into practical substance.

For such unrealistic dreams, more bureaucrats, more money, and more governmental agencies were added. The nation's wealth made such growth possible, but it did not materialize the airy legislative goals.

President Reagan attempted to glorify the private sector, as if General Motors were greater than the U.S. government. Again — look at American history! Businessmen did virtually anything to maximize profits, including bribery, fraud, immoral acts, monopoly, and price-fixing, until such cutthroat business practices were finally curbed by reform movements around the turn of the century and thereafter. Times have changed, though, so that ethics have a central place in today's business practices.

I believe that the government should regulate business, because the government represents public interest, and the private sector is not the guardian of the public interest.

We should perhaps reflect upon the inordinate growth of government our nation has witnessed, despite America's long tradition of Jeffersonian attitudes, which asserted that "government governs best when it governs least."

The U.S, government started as an opponent of monarchy, and anti-governmentalism has been a continuing theme for that reason. Since then, however, the American people have witnessed an unprecedented growth in the federal bureaucracy. Such irony exists because American society evolved, and during the New Deal/New Frontier/Great Society period, people realized that the government which governed least was not necessarily the best. During those years, big government delivered many benefits to the nation as a whole: a higher standard of living, a more egalitarian society, a more compassionate citizenship, and finally, a lesson on the positive role of central government that should not to be undervalued.

What we have to do is to preserve government as the most precious of human possessions and make it work effectively and efficiently. In 1887, Woodrow Wilson wrote, "it is getting harder to run a constitution than to frame one…." after publishing his popular treatise "Congressional Government," which attacked the fragmented and irresponsible committee system in Congress. We should emphasize the art of managing the government — a much more difficult task than writing legislation — and public management should be recognized as an important field of academic and professional accomplishment.

The recent decline in public regard for government is a dangerous indicator of a worrisome trend.

The Reagan presidency did many good things for this nation, but it has done some harm. We should protect the image of government because the decline of respect for government may prove cancerous to the nation's political system in the long run.

CHAPTER 22

A Korean-American Life in Washington/Literary Activities

Being a Korean-American poet and writer would be a very solitary thing without efforts to establish connections, workshops and readings. So, in the Washington area, I organized the Korean Poets and Writers Group in 1990 and the Korean-American Poets Group in 2003. I have been organizing poetry activities for decades. Back in the 1980s, I created a series of poetry readings at the Korean YMCA, and invited famous Korean poets and writers to the YMCA to read and lecture. One most memorable writer was Mr. Yong-Ik Kim from Pittsburgh. With his help, I produced a full-page interview for the Outlook section of the *Washington Post*, which was reprinted in the *Japan Times* (January 27, 1986) and other newspapers.

Kim was an American literary success story. Arriving in the United States in 1948, he spoke only broken English. And yet Kim became a major writer of American fiction. Born and raised in the seaport town of Choongmoo (another name, Tongyoung) in South Korea, Kim based his stories on his experiences in his native South Korea and on the experiences of Orientals in the United States generally. After studying English literature in Tokyo in the early 1940s, he resisted his father's wish that he become a lawyer and came to the United States to continue studying English literature at Florida Southern College and then at the University of Kentucky and the University of Iowa's Writers Workshop. Kim identified himself as a "misfit" in a bureaucratic and mechanical society, although he said he tried hard to be an "adjusted misfit."

In his work — which was published in English and included roughly 30 published short stories, four novels, two one-act plays and a full-length drama — he said he was "drawn to life untouched by modern mechanism and conformity and standardization." He neither owned nor knew how to drive a car, did not have a phone and a television set until 1974, 10 years before I invited him to the Korean YMCA lecture. His work often involves simple tales of people who could be his relatives, looking for universal meaning in faraway provincial settings.

In addition to writing, Kim taught fiction writing at the University of California at Berkeley. When he was visiting the Korean YMCA, he was teaching at Duquesne University in Pittsburgh.

Kim became an American citizen in 1976. His work appeared in the *Atlantic*, the *New Yorker*, the *Hudson Review* and the *Sewanee Review*. He received a grant from the National Endowment for the Arts for his creative writing.

My interview with him touched on many of the issues faced by Korean-Americans, especially those with an artistic bent. It was entitled, "Finding Voice in a Foreign Tongue":

Q: Did you have a great ambition to be a writer in the United States?

A: I never thought about becoming a professional writer. In this country, I had an adjustment problem, and I was very lonely, so every morning I got up and I started to write — three hours every day. My roommate asked me, "What are you doing?" and I responded, "I am writing a book." He said, "If you get your work published in America, I'll give you $500. Even for American writers, it's very hard to break into that racket." But I wrote every morning about three hours all my life.

Q: What did you write at that time?

A: I missed my hometown, and so I tried to capture that emotion and passion of Korean children through my work. I write what I feel, and my playmates in my childhood come to me very naturally. They were poor people even by Korean standards. Some didn't have fathers. Their mothers were out all day peddling homegrown bean sprouts. Some were retarded. But we chased the runaway kites under the blue sky. We sometimes slipped and fell in cow dung, but we always got up laughing, chasing those kites. I like my hometown largely because it is untouched (by) modern mechanism and conformity.

Q: What was the first story you published?

A: I wrote about "The Wedding Shoes." A butcher's son falls in love with the beautiful daughter of the shoemaker who refused the marriage proposal from the young man. When you write a story in this country, a story of Korea, you have to have some universal appeal. Although my father was not (a) butcher, I felt that I was a butcher's son. When you start to think about when (the) first Americans came to this country, they had to fight Indians and so on. All of us are butcher's sons. So I thought, perhaps American readers can understand the Korean themes, the beautiful wedding shoes from the butcher's son's point of view.

Q: How long did you spend writing and rewriting the story?

A: Actually that story took two months. I was working on one book, *The Happy Days* and I finished it and sent it to New York, but it always returned to me. One day I was so discouraged, and so I just listened to music the whole day and I didn't eat. Somehow the image of wedding shoes came to my mind. I thought if I capture those wedding shoes, the elusive wedding shoes, maybe I can write a real story.

But I felt very hungry, so I went to a grocery store and after spending so much money sending my manuscript I didn't have much money. I went to the meat counter, and I said, "a few slices of meat, please." He picked a huge hunk of meat and wrapped it up and marked it 30 cents. I said I only ask you for two slices, three slices. He said, "Oh, that's okay." I went to the cashier. The cashier looked at the package and looked at me, but she didn't say anything.

Every time I returned, somehow the package seemed to grow bigger, but still he charged me 30 cents. For two months when I was working on "The Wedding Shoes," I had a very high protein diet. Before that I used to eat only doughnuts and coffee. He was a butcher, and I wrote the story from the butcher's son's point of view.

Q: Was your book finally published?

A: Yes, by Little Brown.

Q: T.S. Eliot went to England and became a British subject and never returned to the United States. Do you think you can stay the rest of your life in this country? Do you plan to die in this country?

A: To me, it doesn't matter where you live. I always think about Korea and I write about Korea mainly, and what's the difference whether I stay in Korean mountains to write about Korea or live in America writing about Korea? I don't see any difference, because my mind returns to Korea always. Actually I shouldn't say return, because my playmates in my hometown are always within me, not the books.

Q: You are now a famous writer. Are you rich?

A: This year I received a fellowship from National Endowment for the Arts, and also I was commissioned to work on a teleplay. I made money, but I don't know, when I think about my Korean village. My playmates came from very poor homes. My father was a small landlord, and they used to call my family rich. Of course, when I went to Seoul and Japan and America, my family was not that rich. This materialistic aspect of life doesn't interest me that much. Just to write.

When I write one good short story, I'm always excited and that story I created comes back to me again and again. I write about human success in the rapture of darkness. This is my happy time. Every time I write, I feel good.

Q: The United States has changed dramatically since 1948. What have been the most dramatic changes you have noticed?

A: First, as a teacher, I noticed change. During the Vietnam War I started to teach in America. When I gave a grade of D or F, my students behind my back called me "that damned gook." But now they're interested in Oriental culture and would like to learn something about Oriental people. As a writer, publishers and editors talk about serious literature, but when you and I look at books at the store, it is only lip service. For commercial reasons, they are not interested in publishing stories that are set in Korean villages, because they feel that they cannot make money perhaps.

Q: You spent several years in your early college life in Japan. What was that like?

A: I went to a college in Tokyo, Japan, during the Second World War. The first American air attack—I criticized the Japanese war effort and was put in jail. Four or five days later, when the Japanese chief of police passed my cell, I told him, "I've been in here for four days without even being questioned."

When the chief of police left the jail, I heard him asking the guard, "What is his name?" The guard said, "He's a Korean." The chief didn't say anything further. After that, the guard came over with a bucketful of cold water and threatened to pour the water into my cell. It was a cold winter. I had to sleep on the wooden floor. My cellmate, a Japanese vagrant caught stealing money from a donation box, hit me and asked me to apologize to the guard. I was frightened. I apologized to the guard. I felt very bad about saying "Sorry" to the guard, and I realized I would never become a hero.

Q: Why do you live here, even though you miss and love your home country?

A: I always like a strange town where no one knows me and (I can) run around seeing strange places and meeting strange people. Also, in small countries like Korea and Japan, human relations are so tightly knitted that I wanted to be liberated. But away from Korea, I always think of Korea. When I returned to my hometown three years ago, I lost my way to the home in which I grew up and had to ask someone how to get there. With all sorts of new buildings and new paved roads, the town has changed a great deal. After that experience, I don't get homesick as much as I used to, and I begin to realize that Pittsburgh is my home. Sometimes my relatives in my hometown send me a package of Korean food. When I open the package and find the dry squid and kelp, anchovies, bracken shoots and ginseng, I can smell my hometown's seafront. I can smell the Korean earth. Then I laugh and sigh.

* * * * *

Voice of America, and My Voice

In 2003, I spoke on the Voice of America's "New American Voices" on the subject of Korean-American life. It was a centennial celebration of the first Korean immigrants to Hawaii sugar plantations. They left Korea in December 1902 and arrived at Hawaii in January 1903 by ship. They were the first Korean-Americans.

"All-in-all I am positive towards U.S. society and the U.S. government and the American people as the leading nation and the leading people of this world society in the 21st century," I told the host. "Sometimes I see the glorious aspect of American life, sometimes I see some of the tragic, or arrogance-of-power side, sometimes I see the human-being dominated, or law-dominated society, and I try to reflect this in my poems."

On the 1960s and 1970s: "I was so attracted to the United States. What made the United States great was that kind of vitality: the civil rights movement for human equity and equality; the environmental movement for the man and nature relationship; and the anti-Vietnam war movement, an unjust war the young people tried to stop. I think all these three movements that I observed in the first part of my American life were unforgettable and I believe that such power and such forces still remain somewhere in this country."

On discrimination in the United States: "Well, I shouldn't say this, but during my Pentagon experiences NATO people couldn't come to my office, or they were led to another room, skipping my office. I felt some bias and prejudice still existing in this country. All these kinds of things are still in my memory, but I still say this country is greater than any other country in accepting and accommodating foreign people, and that it is the land of hope and opportunities."

On poetry: "It's more or less personal poetry, it's basically my life, my 30-some years of American life reflected in 50 poems. I try to show my anger and my happiness, my pathos, almost everything is there. But poetry and literature is what I have been dependent on in a sense to sustain my life."

The host said this about my poetry: "One of Mr. Choi's early poems, entitled "MY SAIL," shows his dichotomy of feeling on leaving Korea to come to America."

"A gull/and solitude with the solidity of a thing./My sail shines fresh venturing along/In the shadow of the Pacific./What am I searching for in a distant land?/What have I cast off in my native land?/The waves are playing, the winds whistle,/And the mast bows and creaks./Alas! I am searching for happiness!/Below the soul a stream of glistening azure/Between the vast expanse of the sky and the waters."

"For the past three years," the host continued, "Dr. Choi has been commuting from his home in a Washington suburb to Seoul, Korea, where he is a professor and chairman of the environmental policy program in the University of Seoul's Graduate School of Urban Sciences. He accepted the job, he says, because he has an aged mother in Korea, and as the eldest son he has a duty to take care of her. Dr. Choi says that after 30 years in the United States, he still embodies strong Korean, as well as American, values."

"I've been Korean in the sense that I am going back to Korea to take care of my mother, that's the Korean aspect, filial piety, but I enjoy my freedom of thinking and freedom of expression, as a poet and writer I appreciate the country I am living in."

"Yearn Hong Choi is married to an American-Korean woman, and has two grown children, both of whom work on Wall Street, the financial district of New York. He says their values are quite different from his."

"(laughs) Oh, yes. They are American. They are not Korean-American, they are totally American. It's a totally different world they live in. This is their country, English is their mother tongue. Probably the language and the value systems they acquired from kindergarten and all the way… They are good American citizens."

"Yearn Hong Choi, who considers himself to be both Korean and American, finds it somehow ironic that in Korea he himself is often seen as an American."

"Well, some people think I am a foreigner, some people think I am too pro-American, but it's all right with me. I have two countries I'm living in. And maybe this is still much freer and more comfortable than my home country. Both sides have virtues and things I care about and value highly. I've been very fortunate to live in two worlds, and get good things from two worlds. I appreciate my life, I thank the society I have been in, and I'm grateful particularly in this centennial year for Korean immigration."

* * * * *

Short Story in Short Story International, Indiana University Alumni Magazine and a College Textbook

Yong Ik Kim suggested I write a short story after he read *A Woman's Death.* My next short story was *Bloomington, Fall 1971,* about the love of two Korean students at Indiana University, that was first published as the cover story of *Indiana University Alumni Magazine* (1985) and then reprinted in *Short Story International* (1988), and reprinted for a college textbook in *Intercultural Journeys through Reading and Writing* edited by Marilyn Smith Layton (HarperCollins, 1991). In the story, the young man's mother urges him to stop seeing her, because she is from a different family background. After agonizing hours, he makes a decision to marry her. My short story was circulated among all Indiana University graduates and appeared in *Short Story International* with the world's great contemporary writers. It was my great honor, as were the textbook discussion questions following my story. They included: "What Korean cultural assumptions, values, and attitudes does Yearn Hong Choi establish in his story?" And "What American influences play a part in his eventual problems over Kyung Sook? What becomes the central conflicts that he must face and make choices about?" My reflections in fiction on love between Korea and America had begun to stimulate the reflections of others!

Gwendolyn Brooks and Reed Whittemore

In the 1980s I met Edward Reed Whittemore, Poet Laureate of Maryland, while teaching at the University of Maryland. I also met Gwendolyn Brooks, the Pulitzer Prize-winning poet. Those who know poetry will know Whittemore and most educated Americans will recognize Brooks, a famous poet and poetess. Both poets served as Library of Congress Poetry Consultants. Later the title of "poetry consultant" was changed to the more prestigious-sounding "Poet Laureate."

When my first poetry book in English, *Autumn Vocabularies*, was published by the Writers' Workshop in Calcutta, India, Gwendolyn Brooks sent me a poem, "Yearn Hong Choi." I used it in my poetry book. She encouraged and cheered me to continue my poetry writing. I miss her.

Yearn Hong Choi

Here is a man consciously in the world.
He looks, he sees, he executes, he deplores.
He capsulizes! He magnifies!

He knows that one of the ingredients of human
Existence is infamy, that another is cold cruelty,
That another is weakness.
But he is also aware of positives — and of nuances
That whisper of potential.
He is a skillful wielder of language.
He uses language with sensitive enjoyment, with
Canny respect.
Yearn Hong Choi is a new influencer and enhancer.

Here are Gwen's letters to me. She wrote them in long-hand, and I reproduce them here in her honor, all written from Chicago, Illinois:

June 28, 1986

My goodness, Yearn! — how proud I am that you wrote about me at such length! To think that people in Korea are reading about me this very month! THANK YOU!

One of my real regrets is that I was not able to present you at the Library of Congress (you had to go out of town that day). How the audience would have loved you!

I have talked with the editor of Third World Press. He says he has had financial troubles galore, and is not publishing just now, except on a partnership basis: that means, the publisher pays half the expenses, the author pays half, and each keeps half the edition, selling it as desired. I doubt you'll want to assume such a burden, so I recommend you try another publisher — perhaps one of the Washington publishers. Ethelbert Miller there, at Howard University, knows all the Washington literary contingents and may be able to help you.

If you decide to try another publisher, ask Third World to return your manuscript.

Meanwhile, here is the little introduction I promised.

(Her poem was printed in my poetry book, *Autumn Vocabularies,* published in 1990.)

Have a glorious summer!

Warm regards,
Gwen Brooks

August 21, 1986

Hi! Hi! There!

    I cannot tell you how proud I am that you wanted to write about me, — at such length! Thanks for introducing me to Korean readers!

    Your work is so beautiful that — sooner or later — it is certain to achieve the reception, the attention it deserves.

Sincerely,
Gwendolyn Brooks

October 5, 1986

Dear Yearn—

    Thank you for this long, long, warm-hearted review!

    I must tell you that "We Real Cool" was written not for a Little Rock girl, but in recognition of seven boys in my own Chicago neighborhood whom I saw shooting pool during school time — in a poolroom called "Baylock's" on the corner of 74th and Cottage Grove. I enclose for you a copy of the poem.

    Yearn, that word in my tribute to you is not "INFORMY," but INFAMY.

    I like your picture in the article, but I don't like mine! So I'm sending you one, as I'd like you to remember me!!

    Every word I said about you is true, Yearn! You are a very special poet, and a very special person!

    Affectionately,
    Gwen Brooks

We Real Cool
—the pool players, seven at the Golden School

We real cool. We
Left school. We
Lurk late. We
Strike straight. We
Sing sin. We
Thin gin. We
Jazz June. We
Die soon.

November 6, 1989

Hi, there!

I'm in California for two weeks.

Thank you so much for your kind-hearted invitation to Korea!

I'd love to see it — and speak there. But all of next summer is pre-obliged!!!

Can't go. But it is so dear of you to want me to come.

Gratefully,
Nevertheless—
Gwen Brooks

The above letter was in response to my invitation on behalf of the World Congress of Poets in the summer of 1990.

October 20, 1990

Hi, Yearn!

This beautiful book! "Autumn Vocabularies" — even the title is exquisite! Thank you! — for this gift of lovely poems, and for letting my poem salute to you inside!

Congratulations!

And BRAVO!

Love and Pride—
Gwen Brooks

* * * * *

Not many people who aren't already poetry aficionados will recognize Edward Reed Whittemore, Jr. His friends call him Reed. I am proud to know him. He is a good poet and writer, and very sympathetic to a Korean poet like myself.

Born in 1919 in New Haven, Connecticut, he graduated from Yale University and taught at Carleton College in Minnesota and University of Maryland at College Park. I met him when he was The Poetry Consultant for the Library of Congress. He was friendly and read my poems. We had many lunch hours together near the Library of Congress and later at College Park when he retired from that job becoming both the Poet Laureate of Maryland and an emeritus professor at the University of Maryland.

So, here I was, befriending a member of American Academy of Arts and Sciences with a distinguished record in the field. Among his awards were the Harriet Monroe prize from *Poetry* Magazine (Chicago), the Award of Merit of the American Academy of Arts and Letters, a major grant from the National Institute of the Arts, and a Guggenheim Fellowship to complete his acclaimed biography of the poet William Carlos Williams. From 1964-65, he served as The Poetry Consultant to the Library of Congress. He was reappointed to the same position for 1984-1985.

On one occasion, he introduced me to Allen Ginsberg. I invited both Whittemore and Ginsberg to the World Poets' Congress in Seoul in the early 1990s and ended up translating Ginsberg's famous poetry book, *Howl*, into the Korean language and publishing it in Seoul. He later invited me to his apartment in New York City where I had the honor of mingling with that "Beat" poet or "dirty old poet."

Here is my interview with Whittemore, conducted in his office, the Poetry Room of the Library of Congress, and printed in the *Chosun Ilbo* on March 16, 1985. Every word is still precious to me.

A Korean Poet interviews an American Poet

Q: Why do you write poems? This is the age of prose.

A: I write poems because they make sense. My father was a doctor, but I became a poet. I don't regret it. I have been writing poems for 45 years. I started to write and publish my poems in my freshman year at Yale. My three poems and two stories were published in *Yale Literature*, and later I became the editor of the *Yale Lit*. Materialism prevails in the United States. But I separate myself from materialism. Many poets separate themselves from materialism. This is the age of prose, but prose does not reject verse. The two make good contrast.

Q: What is a poem? Do you have your own definition? Defining poetry is more difficult than writing poems.

A: I don't have my own definition. Poetry is some kind of expression of feeling. It is very hard to define. Carl Sandburg once defined poems romantically. He looked at poetry as the birds flying in the sky.

Q: Walt Whitman was the first, or one of the first great poets in the United States. His poems did aim at building democracy in this new nation in the mid-19th century. His poems also did aim at raising patriotism to this nation. In recent years, I have seen Robert Lowell, Galway Kinnell, last year's Pulitzer poet, and Allen Ginsberg, among today's leading poets. Who is today's Walt Whitman?

A: Allen Ginsberg. He is writing his poems in the Whitman style.

Q: But today's American poems tend to be private and individualistic. They seem to be the majority. How do you view the private or privatized poems?

A: Lowell opened the so-called "confessional poetry." I like Lowell, but today's poems are much too private, and much too special. Some poems may serve psychiatric therapy to the poets who wrote them. I don't know.

Q: Erica Jong's works became best-sellers. How do the so-called private works become best-sellers?

A: Her works are much more private. They are sex. Sex is communal. You don't need to communicate.

Q: You are a social critic in your poems. Did you participate in any anti-war demonstrations in the 1960s, or write poems against Vietnam War?

A: I did participate in some demonstrations. I published a poem against bombing in the *New Yorker* in the 1960s.

Q: Are you related to Henry David Thoreau?

A: (smile) I was told Thoreau was related to my mother's side. I visited Walden Pond twice. It is now too much commercialized.

Q: You are a New Englander by birth but you are also a long-time Minnesotan, and a Washingtonian. Which place is the most influential in your poetry?

A: My hometown, New Haven, is a town of middle-class people. My poems on middle-class life originated from my college days. My poems on nature are due to my Minnesota life. My children were born and raised in Minnesota, and they live in Minnesota. Washington offers me urban life.

Q: Any of your children write poems?

A: No. My oldest is an artist.

Q: Who are your favorite poets?

A: Ezra Pound, T.S. Eliot, and William Carlos Williams. They all are my favorite poets. They also influenced my poetry. At Yale, with my roommate, I started *Furioso*, a poetry magazine. As the editor of the poetry magazine, I corresponded with these poets and invited them to contribute their poems to *Furioso*.

Q: How did they differ from one another?

A: Pound is the intelligent poet known as an "imagist." He was a socialist. He was an unusual man. He sent me a poem composed of four quotations from four U.S. Presidents' speeches. I used it, because I invited him, but I was shocked. The Great Depression deeply affected his life, poetry and thinking. I never met Eliot. He was already in England. His poems were philosophic documents. Williams was an aesthetic poet.

Q: Who is closer to you?

A: In my basic approach, I'm closer to Eliot.

Q: But you are the famous biographer of William Carlos Williams, aren't you?

A: Yes, I am. I was physically close to Williams. We corresponded for a long time. He was a good poet, but was not fashionable then compared to Eliot and Pound. He is fashionable now. His short poems are the best. Did you read "Red Wheelbarrow?" New Jersey is now constructing the William Carlos Williams Center. I have not heard yet whether Missouri or England is constructing a T.S. Eliot Center.

Poetry Reading in the Library of Congress

On April 28, 1994, I was invited to read my poems in the Library of Congress under the auspices of the Gertrude Clarke Whittall Poetry and Literature Fund. As the first Korean poet who was invited to read my poems, I was deeply honored. The Library of Congress invited Dr. Seung Soo Han, the Ambassador from Korea. He was out of town for his attendance at former president Richard M. Nixon's funeral in California, but deputy ambassador Ki Moon Ban, who later became U.N. Secretary General in 2006, came to my poetry reading and delivered a short congratulatory speech. Some of the poems I read are below.

I like to think of Korean-American poets and writers as a forest — a forest with its many different elements of nature coming together to make one. All kinds of trees and plants, creeks, rocks, birds, deer, morning glories, waterfalls, and sounds of water – a diversity of trees or plants, squirrels, and deer make up the forest of Korean-American literature. Diversity makes one picturesque forest.

Korean-American poets and writers have a great sense of loss and sense of deprivation. The loss is the loss of their home country, their mother tongue, their relatives and friends, and their past. Literature fills the void or the loss. Yong Ik Kim came to the United States as a young student after the Korean War, and wrote many short stories in prestigious literary magazines such as the the *New Yorker* and the *Atlantic. Happy Days, the Diving Gourd, Blue in the Seed, Love in Winter,* and *The Shoes from Yang San Valley,* all novels, were published by major publishing houses such as Little Brown, Alfred Knopf, and Doubleday. *The Happy Days* was selected as one of the outstanding juvenile novels by the *New York Times* in 1965. His short stories were selected as some of the best short stories in America in the 1960s and 1970s. All his creative writings were based upon his memories of childhood and adolescent days in his hometown on the coastal area of the South Sea. He treasured everything in his hometown and attempted to write about it. He never finished the retrieval of his memories.

Yonghill Kang's *Grass Roof* was a sensational novel of the 1930s and 1940s. Richard Kim's *Martyred* was a powerful work in the 1960s, and Chang Rae Lee's *Native Speaker* was one of the best selling serious novels in the 1990s in the United States. Linda Sue Park received the coveted John Newberry Medal for children's books in 2002. There are many rising Korean-American stars among the second and third generation writers.

Cathy Song's *Picture Bride* received the Yale Younger Poets Award in 1982.

Nam Soo Park soothed his painful immigrant's life with his imagist poems. He concealed his frustration in his poems. He came to the United States as an immigrant when he was 51. He could not speak

English very well, but was a proud poet. "Seagull" was one of his most representative poems, but "Guggenheim Museum" and "Daytona Beach" showed how he viewed his new world.

Korean immigrants were sometimes murdered in the urban ghettos and this, too, was reflected in Korean-American literature. Korea Town in Los Angeles was one target and victim of the Los Angeles riots. Ko Won disclosed the Koreans' anger in his LA elegy and dark tears. Elsie Kim identified them as the homeless. Sang Hee Kwak lamented the tragedy of September 11 in New York City.

Insofar as Korean-American literature is based on sorrow, nostalgia, pathos, yearning, and tears over joy, laughter, victory and happiness in a new land, it reminds us that the new land is still very foreign to the first-generation Korean immigrants. Some resorted to Christian literature as a comfort to the people with sorrow. Oscar Wilde said, "sorrow is the most beautiful thing in the human heart." Yearn Hong Choi is "Going Home" constantly.

We all together make one forest.

In the Library of Congress, I read my poems in Korean, and the Poet Laureate read my poems in English. That is a tradition of the Library of Congress poetry reading. Several Nobel Laureates did read their poems in their mother tongues, and their American friends read their poems in English.

Russia

Peeling the skin of an onion,
Another skin is shown.
Peeling that skin,
Yet another remains.
The golden onion dome
Upon which the cross lies,
And a big star above the cross
Under the star,
There are people of many kinds
Who love Pushkin
Over Marx and Lenin — don't feel sad,
Even if life is betraying you.

At the Atlantic

I leave for the sea
To find something
I never find in the inland office,
Apartment and woods.
The sea is always there
In my cousin's distance
With vitality, rhythm,
Poetic organization.
The sea runs high,
The fleets of waves are beautiful, and
I am approaching the edge of the sea.
Again I return to my virgin sail on the Atlantic
With loneliness, insecurity, a few silver coins
In my pocket.
How young I was compared to the depth
And space of the sea!
I walked into the sea and reached a new continent
Of classic Renaissance, the plain of Eurasia,
And the last port-of-call, my little country.
The night, midnight loses vitality,
O, no, the sea invades the night.
More than philosophy in our brain,
More than thoughts of philosophy
Dwells on the waves of the triumphant shell,
Jean Cocteau!
In between Newton's poetic expression of science
And scientific expression of poetry,
We write each other of human yearning,
And send out letters to the sea
Where foam flowers scatter them in the wind.
However, the words are floating on the sea
And never reach the other side,
And then we come to sleep in different lands,
Island and continent, to dream

To find what we lost
After we departed sometime ago.
And whole the sea remains to fill its destiny.
The sea is alive
With great vitality, rhythm.
Poetic organization.
The sea runs high,
The fleets of waves are beautiful
In washing out our wounded yearning,
Words, fish, night and yearning soul.

The Arizona Desert

Even at high noon
I cannot face this barren field:

The sun, which cremated the
Dead
And left only white bones,
Is still bright as the Inca's

There a crow spreads his wings—
His wings really black
And his beak really red

Cactus endured an empty year
With scarce summer showers;
Birds and chipmunks build
Their homes inside

Indians make jellies
From the cactus flowers
And God happily lays out
A silver mine
Under this cactus field

For a Reunion

30 years have passed away
without our notice.
Once we shake hands with each other
In the corner,
The years are equated by the moment
After our hug.
Our past and yearning for each other become more
Beautiful flowers in our heart.
Past tense of young and relentless wandering, love and pain
In this new land is replaced by
The present tense
Of rare purity.
"How could I forget you?"
You have been in my safe all the years.
A few more drinks offer joy and ease;
Life is short and art is long,
Then long years could be shorter.
"Don't feel bad!"
We are still young,
Years come to our memory
Like a port I visited in the south sea.
…All that glitters is not gold…
All that glitters is our growth
And yearning in long distance.

Will

Rewriting a will written in thought
That it is regretful even to
Die once so
Shouldn't die twice.
Cremate me.

No need for a wooden casket.
No need for a tombstone.
No need for a séance.
After two generations,
Who will visit the grave?

If buried on a mountain in Choongchung province,
Perhaps four generations later
There may be children stuttering Korean
Wandering the homeland mountains.
Flesh will decompose to assimilate with dirt.
Calcareous bones buried underground
Verify one's existence?

Never mind, children.
Burn the body in hot firewood. Burn it all.
Burn till no organic substance will remain.
When a handful of ashes remains,
Scatter them over the waves of the Atlantic.
Death is only meaningful
In the memories of
The surviving ones.
So it is.
Memory is drawing up
Of the death and the life of the dead
From the surviving ones.
Like drawing up water from a well
Not from some country's cemetery.

Hawaii

The sea is in the mirror
And the white doves are in my verandah.
My room is on the eleventh floor.

* * * * *

Second Poetry Reading in the Library of Congress

In January 2003, I was invited to read my poems at the Library of Congress a second time, this time on the celebration occasion of the centennial year of Koreas' laborers' landing in the Hawaii sugar plantations in the early 20th century. In the same year, I edited *Surfacing Sadness: A Centennial of Korean-American Literature* (Homa and Sekey Books). Here are some of the poems I read, many reflecting on my American life.

Journey to Korea

Even though only an empty house
Awaits me, I go.
I beg pardon to my ancestors,
Buried in my family cemetery
Up in the mountains.
I beg for forgiveness; a son living abroad
So long in a foreign land.

Black Korean

The Korea man moved to Hawaiian sugar plantation
At the turn of the century,
and then to Mexico's henequen field,
and finally moved to Cuba's sugar plantation
to make a few dollars.

His grandson, I met in the District of Columbia,
only knew that his grandpa was a Korea man,
but did not know why he was in Cuba.
The old man was supposedly in the hermit kingdom.

The Korea man fell in love with a black woman in Cuba,
And had a son, and his son moved to Miami as a refugee,
then to the District of Columbia.

Jose Suh, I know, has an odd last name.
The Chosun's seed was not just planted in Cuba.
It was also planted in the Central Asia desert,
and the cold wind of Sakhalin
as well.

I see a Korea man's anger, frustration, love
and affection in the black of his grandson.
I see the demise of the Chosun kingdom in a Black-Korean-
American from Cuba,
and the Korean's odyssey.

Reminiscence

A certain coquettish Korean girl
Is my only memory of my Indiana University.
Oh, how flirtatious she was!
I cannot even begin.

She sang always, dreaming of
Being an opera singer someday.
I applauded her dream.

By time and tide
I am older and wiser since my university days.
Even if I see her now
I doubt I would blush as I used to so often then.

My heart yearns for those carefree days—
The innocent days of my youth so long ago—
Wishing to become as a young man once again.
The beautiful campus is still vivid in my memory.
I wonder if the splendor of the green field
Is still the same.
Music by Bach that she and I used to appreciate
May still permeate the fresh air on campus.
There was a beautiful prelude of a young couple.
There was nothing but an overture of young lovers' opera.

Poet's Wife

Pitiful woman!
Being a poet's wife is terrible to her!
Why didn't she realize
Marrying a poet would be a sorrow?
Housing a man searching for a new meaning
All the time is not at all easy to a woman.
What kind of crime did she commit before this life?

Do you know the poet's wife must be
Not only the guardian of his son and daughter,
But also the guardian of him?
It can be fun, hilarious to a certain woman!

The man is supposed to be a monk,
The man is supposed to be a moon walker.
He comes down to the Earth by accident

She gives a son and a daughter to a dreamer.
They become anti-poetic young man and woman.

Oh, how wonderful it is!
An angel from heaven takes care of a pitiful man,
And thus makes this world brightly meaningful.

CHAPTER 23

Korean-American Life in Washington/The Korean Democracy Movement: Before and After 1987

The Korean-American community did not exist when I first came to the Washington area in 1981. There were just a handful of Korean churches, grocery stores and restaurants. Now, there are two Korean community centers: one in Annandale and another in Centerville. Koreans are now one of the largest minority groups in Fairfax, Virginia. There is one Korean-American school board member and many with influence on the congressional elections, both among Democrats and Republicans. Regionally, we have two daily newspapers — the *Korea Times* and the *Korea Daily*, plus one weekly magazine, the *Korea Monitor*. One major television network (NBC) even has a Korean lady as an anchor. Virginia Cha is an anchor/reporter for CNN.

The problem is that Korean-Americans are too often isolated as an ethnic group, or assimilated completely. It is not always easy to enter into the so-called "mainstream" America. Many new arrivals end up isolating themselves. But then some second-generation Korean-Americans ignore their heritage completely. Many feel they do not need the Korean community or the Korean churches. There is a happy medium. That, at least, is what I strive for.

I had a poetry reading in the Korean community in Spring of 2008. I tried to get a couple of lines printed in the *Washington Post's Literary Calendar* in its Book World, but failed. A Korean Buddhist Temple, Borimsa at Fairfax, organized the 49th day ceremony for the victims of the Virginia Tech killings in 2007. I tried to get a couple of lines printed in the *Washington Post's Religion Page Saturday*, but failed.

I thought they were newsworthy but the *Washington Post* did not think that way. The Korean-American people who aimed at the mainstream could be frustrated. The urban riots in American cities in the 1960s were erupted from the African-American people's frustration. So my concerns about the Korean-American community can be a serious one: Is it a self-isolating move? Or is it an acceptable move? Depending upon who views from what angle, this can be a serious issue.

Over the years, since I shared their democratic and anti-authoritarian views, I became friendly with those who fought the authoritarian regime in Korea. Washington was and is a political town. Human rights and civil rights-oriented American organizations were also interested in the democracy movement in South Korea and sympathetic to them.

In one Autumn evening in 1981, Rev. George Ogle visited town and made a speech for the Korean congregation at an American church in Washington, D.C. located at the border of D.C. and Maryland. I was asked to serve as an impromptu interpreter for him. He was a famous American Christian missionary kicked out of Korea by the Park Chung-hee government in 1974 for his political activities "agitating" the Korean workers. That was my first real contact with the Korean organizations concerned with Korean democracy and freedom in Washington, D.C., even though I had frequently written political commentaries against the authoritarian government in Korean language newspapers in Los Angeles and Philadelphia since the 1960s.

After President Park Chung-hee was assassinated by his Korean CIA chief in 1979, another Army General, Chun Doo-hwan, assumed control of the Korean government. In the 1970s and 1980s, Korean freedom fighters were expressing their concern for democracy in Korea to the White House and the Congress. I still remember Rev. George Ogle's impressive speech: "I am seeing Jesus' face in the faces of struggling Korean workers at Inchon harbor." He truly viewed himself as a missionary for Korean workers. Since that night, I translated the statements and speeches of the Korean democracy movements from Korean into English. I disseminated them to the U.S. President, the Congress, and civil rights-oriented interest groups.

Rev. Moon Tong-hwan was among the first, if not the first, Korean to seek exile in Washington, D.C. in 1982 after Gen. Chun's coup. My friends and I would gather for a prayer meeting once a week with Rev. Moon, and later they proposed to start a church in the American church in Washington, D.C. where Rev. George Ogle made his speech once. I was anxious to start a church for Rev. Moon, because we were concerned about his livelihood. His American wife and young children needed financial help, first of all. We organized the Korean Presbyterian Church in Washington, D.C.

In time, the Korean Presbyterian Church became the center of the South Korean democracy and freedom movement in Washington, D.C. Professor Han Wan-sang of Seoul National University's Sociology Department was the second major exile figure to come to town. He was a popular speaker on Biblical interpretations of the Korean political situation at the church. Mr. Kim Dae-jung, the opposition leader and a prominent presidential candidate who opposed Gen. Park, was the third major exile. The church attracted many distinguished opposition party leaders and intellectuals from Korea: Mr. Ham Sok-hon, political philosopher and writer; Professor Lee Moon-young of Korea University; Poet Ko Eun; and the Rev. Kim Jae-joon were among them.

The church played an important role as the Washington haven of these dissident leaders until June 1987. At that long-awaited time the Chun Doo-hwan government yielded to a popular presidential election, as demanded by the opposition forces. It was a turning point for South Korean politics toward democracy. For the first time, I was free to visit my home country that summer. So I ended my long record of activities in pursuit of South Korean democracy — a glorious, successful ending.

That summer, I taught Korean-American students at Yonsei University International Summer School for five weeks. The students' three to six credit hours from Yonsei University were transferable to their American colleges and universities. Many of them were from Ivy League schools. Yonsei University's summer school was popular. The students took courses such as Korean history, Korean literature, Korean language and Korean political economy. I taught a "Comparative Politics: Asian Governments" course in the summer of 1987 and in the summers of the following years. More than teaching,

I enjoyed seeing and living with my mother. Taking care of an aging mother is a son's job, especially the elder son's duty.

At summer school, I felt something strange at Yonsei University which I hadn't experienced previously. This school was founded more than a century ago by American missionaries. And yet, today, Yonsei University students were showing open anti-Americanism to Korean-American students in summer school. It was directed toward those who could not speak Korean fluently. A great majority of the Korean-American students were born in the United States. How could they be expected to speak Korean fluently? Many nationalistic Korean students could not understand the Korean students from the United States. I criticized their narrow tribalism. Why could they not tolerate their fellow Korean students from the other side of the Pacific Ocean? These were people who took extra effort to learn the Korean language, as well as the country's history and government, during the hot and humid summer. They could have stayed home. Why, I wondered, would an alarming number of very prejudiced Koreans students come to Yonsei University, if they were anti-American? Why would they attend a school founded by the Underwood family more than a century before? There were no good answers.

* * * * *

Views on North Korea and U.S. Troops in South Korea

I recently stumbled upon an Op-Ed I wrote for the *Virginian-Pilot* way back in 1977, and was leavened by how little my views on the subject of U.S. troops in South Korea have changed. I have always thought that the withdrawal of U.S. troops makes sense in the long run, but the most important thing is how it is done. The United States cannot leave South Korea in a power vacuum. As the world learned in the 1950s, when the U.S. withdrew precipitously from the region, sparking power bids by North Korea and others, a geopolitical vacuum invites war.

The occasion for the Op-Ed was the sacking of Maj. Gen. John K. Singlaub from his position as Army chief of staff in South Korea for criticizing President Carter's plan to withdraw U.S. troops. Liberal intellectuals shared President Jimmy Carter's decision to reassign the general to another position. Conservative politicians seemed to sympathize with the general. As I put it back then:

The top-secret national Security Council report on the decision to withdraw American troops from South Korea in 1949, recently declassified and made public, demands attention — not that it reveals anything drastically new, but that it still elicits some important lessons. It confirms, above all, that the grave concern of the then-fledgling Republic of South Korea over the premature U.S. troops pullout was fully justified. As it happened, the U.S. move, ironically carried out in spite of South Korea's ardent opposition, led to North Korea's attack on the South a year later, resulting in the Korean War.

It would not be wholly realistic to view the situation today as similar to that in 1949. In fact, several new factors make a lot of difference between then and now. Korean armed forces have grown to reinforce their defense capability substantially. This growing self-reliance in the defense structure has been buttressed by a rapidly developing economy that is backed by political stability under the authoritarian President Park Chung-hee. South Koreans' security consciousness has never been higher than now. The United States, under the 1954 mutual security pact, is committed to the defense of South Korea.

Yet it would be unrealistic to overlook a number of crucial factors that hardly exclude the risk of a renewed war on this volatile peninsula. A premature pullout of the U.S. ground forces could be disastrous. North Korea has massively built its military muscle, poised now for unleashing at any choosing. The North maintains an edge in weapons over the South. It has units trained to wage guerilla warfare. The Communist regime, moreover, remains as unpredictable and adventurous as it was 28 years ago.

And North Korea is militarily allied with the People's Republic of China and the Soviet Union, both of which share borders with it. If either of the two Communist giants is no longer inclined to involve itself overtly in a

North Korean attempt to take over the South by force, there is yet no certainty that either Beijing or Moscow will not support the North even indirectly once Pyongyang unleashes war. Given these circumstances, the war-deterring role of the U.S. ground troops in South Korea cannot be easily discounted, much less dismissed.

For this reason, Carter's intention to phase down U.S. ground troops in Korea over a four-to-five year span deserves careful review. The crucial point lies, not in the planned withdrawal per se, but in how it is going to be done without creating a vacuum, real or seeming, in the precarious balance of military power in Korea. U.S. air power and sea power do not substitute for ground power in terms of effectiveness as a war-deterrent.

I agree to the plan to withdraw. U.S. foreign and military policy should be guided basically by the Monroe Doctrine. However, when any small nation is under attack from a Communist-giant-supported regime, the United States should resort to the Truman Doctrine for international peace and ethics, and for democracy.

North Korea and South Korea should search for peaceful reunification. If the peaceful way is not available, then they should adopt articles of confederation. However, that is far, very far from the possible, unfortunately.

May 29, 1977. p. A21.

* * * * *

The split of the opposition party by Kim Young-sam and Kim Dae-jung in the 1987 presidential election resulted in the victory of former Army General Roh Tae-woo. I was personally disappointed by the former army general's victory. But I enjoyed my freedom to visit Korea in the following summers and to live with my mother who was lonely after my father had passed away in June 1982. Five weeks living with my mother in Seoul made my mother happy. I was happy, too.

Kim Young-sam and Kim Dae-jung each became president in their respective victories, the one in 1992 and the other in 1997. Kim Dae-jung won the Nobel Peace Prize during his presidency. Many of my old friends who I met at the Korean Church in Washington, D.C. became cabinet members and national assemblymen during this period. My role as a critic ended when Korea started its democratization in June 1987 and I enjoyed their victories. Or so I thought. Later, I disagreed with Kim Dae-jung's so-called "sun shine policy" toward North Korea, because the policy amounted to appeasement. Appeasement could not bring any real change to North Korea under a dictatorial rule, I was quite confident.

During a couple of years in the early 1980s when Kim Dae-jung was exiled in Washington, I often visited his Landmark apartment and spent many hours with him. Following is my interview with Kim Dae-jung which was printed in *Korean Roots*, a Los Angeles-based magazine. The interview shows our ideas and thoughts on U.S. foreign policy and South Korea's democratization in 1982. It was conducted in the Korean language so I had the freedom to translate our conversations. It seems a very old story when I re-read it again. Here are some of the highlights.

An Interview with Mr. Kim Dae-jung

I first asked Kim: "You were critical of President Reagan's quiet diplomacy when you arrived at the National Airport last December. The *Washington Post* editorial, in response to your statement, endorsed Reagan's quiet diplomacy. Do you still stand against quiet democracy?"

He said he maintained "the same view against quiet diplomacy. Quiet diplomacy may confuse the world's nations and people. Quiet diplomacy only connects the government to other government leaders, not the general public. How do the world's people know the United States' foreign policy? There is no way of knowing it. U.S. foreign policy should be openly understood by the nations of the world. I don't deny there is some virtue in quiet diplomacy. For example, in my own case, saving my life and rescuing me from a death sentence by arranging for a life sentence, and then exile to the United States, should not and cannot be done by open diplomacy. But the principle of U.S. foreign policy should be known to the people of the world. I don't expect every detailed foreign policy action to be open. But the principles should be open."

Kim spent much time at this moment speaking at U.S. universities including Harvard, Columbia, Princeton and elsewhere urging the United States to stop supporting repressive regimes in the name of anticommunism. "The United States Constitution and the spirit of the United State nation-building should be renewed in U.S. foreign policy toward Korea and other nations," he would urge. "What I mean is the United States should not support dictatorial or authoritarian governments which have alienated and betrayed the majority of the people. The democratic aspiration of the Korean people is enormous. Why does the United States not support Korean democracy? Democracy in Korea is consistent with U.S. interests. The majority of the Korean people support a legitimate government. The majority of the Korean people are alienated from the Korean military government." It was time for a change. The problem seemed to be a kind of policy inertia in Washington. Interestingly to all Koreans, the United States seemed to be genuinely interested in supporting Korean democracy by the late 1950s and early 1960s. But that all changed when Park Chung-hee's coup succeeded in 1961. From that point forward for more than two decades, the U.S. government seemed to support the Korean military government for the sake of economic development and stability. It went along to get along, in the name of anticommunism.

For certain, Kim was appreciative of the Reagan administration's efforts to free him from prison in Korea. But he also credited President Carter, Senator Edward Kennedy, and other Americans who pressed the issue and called upon President Reagan to keep up the discussions. Kim was sure that this pressure on Reagan made the difference. When he met Carter at Emory University the previous month, Kim "expressed my gratitude for his care for my life" and told him, "You will be remembered as the U.S. President who re-established American foreign policy based on human rights. Your policy really lifted the American conscience. You will be remembered for your noble cause for human rights in this 20th century." Kim also recommended the establishment of a human rights center whose awards could rival the Nobel Prize. Sure enough, the Carter Center at Emory was already underway. It may not rival the Nobel Committee for influence, but it is nevertheless an important center of foreign-policy thinking.

I asked Kim to comment on the feeling among many American intellectuals that the Carter presidency was more style than substance. Is he really a great leader? "I think he is, even though I tend to agree that there was more style than substance," Kim responded. "In his early presidential campaign, he said, 'human rights are the heart of the U.S. foreign policy.' I think that sort of statement affected the world's nations at that time. Human right was the spirit of this new nation in 1787. 'Give me liberty, or give me death!' was an expression of the cause of the American people's independence from the British colonial rule. Human rights have been expanded within the nation, but forgotten in its foreign policy for a while. President Carter just renewed it."

Style, not substance? "Style and substance would be better. But style itself is an important element of political leadership. Well, look at President Kennedy's one thousand days in the White House. We still remember him as a leader more for his style than his substance. President Lyndon B. Johnson also substantiated his style."

It seemed now, I observed, that the United States government was more concerned about Korea's stability and security than democracy. Kim found it foolhardy, not to mention counterproductive, if real security is the aim.

"I have heard that kind of reasoning," he said. "It is absurd. Why? National security without democracy is an empty can. There is nothing inside. A good can without any valuable thing inside does not make any sense. National security is and has been endangered by the Korean military government, and the U.S. government, which has been supportive of the Korean military governments. Adolf Hitler's Germany invited communism in East European nations, and the Japanese invasion of Manchuria and mainland China invited communism in China." He saw a similarly unstable situation as long as the United States failed to promote real democracy.

"Hundreds of Korean people who want their lives, liberties, and happiness were sent to prisons. There are many newspapers, political parties, a parliament..... But the newspapers have not published a single article on my forced trip to the United States. The political parties were each made by Army colonels. They cannot criticize the president or his policies. There has been no democratic popular presidential election in South Korea since 1971. The National Assembly is without any meaningful power and authority. These days, many Korean college students stage protests against the military rule in South Korea. They know that their participation in such protest movements will ruin their lives. But they have participated, and will continue to do so. Why do they sacrifice their lives? They want democracy, freedom and social justice."

Maybe the U.S. government simply believed that South Korea is not ready for Western democracy?

"That is ridiculous. I hope it is only a guess. When the United States first opened democracy in 1787, there was not so many literate people and not so many thoughtful people on this continent as today's

South Korean people. I think that South Korea is much better prepared for democracy."

But the Korean people enjoyed economic progress under Park Chung-hee's leadership. Can't Koreans justify a less-than-desirable democracy if their standard of living increases?

"We should distinguish economic progress from economic growth. There has been economic growth in South Korea. The Gross National Product is bigger than ever. But there has been high inflation and gross injustice in the distribution of that wealth. Foreign loans constitute a big portion of the Korean economy. Too much dependence on the foreign market, mainly on the United States and Japan, and too much foreign debt may not be good for the nation's economic well-being in the long run."

On the state of the American public's knowledge of international affairs: "The American people should learn more about world affairs. The national television networks, daily newspapers, and weekly magazines spend much time and space on international affairs. This world is becoming a smaller community. The reality is that this is one Earth. A small planet is connected by new communication and transportation modes. Multinational corporations dominate our markets. For example, General Motors and Toyota have made a joint venture. Under these circumstances, U.S. citizens should know world affairs, because the U.S. is the leader in international affairs. However, to win over the U.S.S.R., the U.S. should gain support from the Third World nations which constitute the majority of the world's nations."

We then spoke about his political ambitions, including some objections to his upcoming fellowship at Harvard, where some felt he would be campaigning rather than engaging in scholarship. "Thomas Jefferson was a politician and scholar. Woodrow Wilson was a scholar and politician. Both are among my favorite American presidents. I am interested in building a democratic nation and culture as advocated by Thomas Jefferson, John Locke, and John Stuart Mill among others.

Who else is your favorite president? I asked. "Andrew Jackson for his democratization of the American political system and process; Abraham Lincoln for his maintaining unity of this nation from the

Civil War; John F. Kennedy for his dream and ambition; and Jimmy Carter for his human rights."

Do you still want to run for the presidency in South Korea? I wanted to know next.

"That is not my concern any more. Democracy in Korea is what I am running for. I believe I was elected as president of South Korea in 1971. Park Chung-hee's Korean CIA chief admitted that in his memoir that I had won the election as the president. There was a series of illegal manipulations of the election results.

Do you plan to go back to Korea? "Korea is my home country. I have every right to go back to my country. I know I am not a criminal. The South Korean government made me a criminal." Even under the present Korean government's rule? "Yes, I am firm about it."

We finally had a more free-wheeling discussion about the ideas underlying politics. How do you define politics? I asked. "Politics is an art, or science of the management of human and social justice. Every citizen's self-fulfillment is the goal of politics." What is your definition of democracy? "Government by the people. Government of the people and for the people is claimed by all 160 nations of the United Nations General Assembly. Government by the people prevails only in 30 nations in Western Europe, Australia, Japan and North America."

This seemed worthy of a few more questions. "Even in American politics, government by the people does not fully exist," I noted. "Many people don't participate in the electoral process. They are apathetic."

"Low-level participation does necessarily mean low quality politics and democracy, because all the qualified citizens are guaranteed the right to run for office and vote for his or her favorite candidate," Kim said. "Low-level participation is less than desirable. However, low-level participation is a kind of choice. Choice is the key element in democracy. In South Korea, there is no choice for the people."

But what if some people are simply uninterested in politics — like most American people seem to me to be? Most college students would say to me at that time that there was no choice between the two major party candidates.

Kim called this "Happy discontent." As he put it: "Reagan and Carter were distinctive candidates. One is a moderate liberal and the other is a typical conservative. They are conservative economic policy advocates." It seemed quite clear to him what the differences were. "Happy discontent" was a fine way to put it.

If Kim had a chance to meet President Reagan, what would he say?

"You are the symbol of American conservatism. You had better conserve the precious national spirit; that is, human rights and democracy, in your foreign policy. The national spirit is well expressed in the Declaration of Independence and the United States Constitution. If your foreign policy with human rights does not work as expected, please don't be disappointed. History will remember the United States' foreign policy even in the case of its defeat. World history will record the glorious and honorable U.S. foreign policy with its novel cause."

Chapter 24

Virginia Cha, Miss America Runner-up/CNN Reporter

I saw her in the Miss America pageant on TV. She was almost crowned. She was the first runner-up. She was Virginia Cha, my friend's daughter in the Maryland suburbs of Washington, D.C. My family, including my daughter, then 11 years old, was proud of her. Of course, she was the pride of every Korean-American.

I finally met her and her family for my column in the *Korea Herald*. My interview article with her below appeared on November 4, 1989 and January 10, 1990 in two installments.

She was still Miss Maryland. Her duties as Miss Maryland kept her busy for one year. Participating in all manner of official Maryland events, from the governor's mansion to the Great Frederick Fair, kept her out of school that year. She planned to go to graduate school the following year.

I was surprised at her good command of the Korean language. When South Korean president Roh Tae-woo visited Washington, she communicated with the president at the Omni Sherham Hotel banquet in fluent Korean. She impressed 1,200 guests. Born in the United States in 1965, she is a graduate of Princeton University, went to Korea as a Fulbright Scholar and studied at Seoul National University and Yonsei University during 1986-1988. She studied modern Korean literature.

Her parents taught her Korean at home. She did not even need Korean language school on Saturdays. She gave due credit to her parents and brother for her language training. She participated in the Seoul Olympics as NBC-TV's assistant producer. Her Korean-American pride, she says, is what drove her to learn Korean so fully.

She became Miss Frederick, and then Miss Maryland, and finally Miss America runner-up with a very short preparation for the fierce

184

competition. She returned to the United States in December 1988 from the Seoul Olympics. In a few months, she entered the beauty competition. Many people who knew her were surprised to see her in the pageant. She earned an ample number of scholarships to pursue her graduate work. She had not decided which school she would attend when I met her. She wanted to be a great TV-news anchor-woman in the future. She liked Walter Cronkite, CBS anchor in the 1950s and 1960s. She also liked Gloria Estefan, the pop music star who overcame all the difficulties in her early life. Contrary to pop music, she impressively played Chopin's Aeolian harp, Etude Opus 25, No. 1 at the beauty pageant.

She told me: "I believe in excellence, and excellence will be rewarded, regardless of race, creed, or color."

To my question, "How do you evaluate yourself?"

She answered, "I am confident to say that my goal is set and I have a conviction to achieve that goal. In that sense, I score myself 9.9 out of 10. I did my best and worked really hard. However, I take care more of the process than the end result. I emphasize the process."

She was Maryland's Junior Miss in 1982.

She said, "Beauty is an attractive quality whoever possesses it. Korean beauty is physically different from American beauty. But beauty is an aesthetic thing. As Mozart's music and Tolstoy's works have been appreciated by all people, so is beauty."

I asked her about the chance of Korean literature coming to the shores of the United States.

She said without hesitation: "I am positive. Translation is a key. Translation is an art, a creative art. I would like to translate some Korean literature — works of Hwang Soon-won, Chung Chi-yong and Kim Young-rang. Korean literature has not been exposed yet to this country.

I met many young Korean-American college students. Some expressed "rejection" from both Korea and the United States. I have cheered them up. My words for them were: "This world is for you. You possess two worlds. You must take advantage of being a Korean-American." Miss Maryland, Virginia Cha, is always a good example of a model youth.

I printed an interview with her in the *Korea Herald*. Following is part of it:

Q: What made you run for the beauty pageant?

A: I don't look at the Miss America contest as a beauty pageant. Good looks are no way to win. The pageant is decided by four different categories: the judges' interview is 30 percent; the talent show is 40 percent; evening gown look and personality is 15 percent; and the swimsuit look is 15 percent. The judges' interview and talent show make 70 percent. That means the Miss America contest is a scholarship program contest. I wanted the scholarship fund for my graduate work, and wanted to improve myself. More than winning, I wanted self-improvement. Eighty-thousand young women participated at local pageants, and then 51 represented 50 states and Washington, D.C. Out of 51, 10 finalists were selected, then 5 and finally the one was selected.

Q: You were selected as Maryland's junior queen in 1982 in your high school days. Was it a stepping stone to Miss America contest?

A: No. I didn't think of the Miss America pageant in 1982. My four years at Princeton gave me confidence to run for Miss America. When asked what her Princeton life was, she said, "I joined a theatrical group, a dancing group, a singing group which toured the nation and cut two albums, a track team, and the student government. I enjoyed my four years there."

Q: After Princeton, you left for Korea. What did you do in Korea?

A: As a Fulbright Scholar, I spent one year and a half at Seoul National University and Yonsei University. I translated works of Korean female poets into English, including Moe Yoon-sook, Kim Nam-jo and Huh Young-ja.

Q: Did you work for the NBC Olympic crew in Seoul?

A: I joined the NBC News Bureau in Seoul for the Olympic coverage. It was April. I was the first Korean-American recruited. I prepared for Korean politics, economy, education, culture and scenic beauty.

Q: Did your Olympic coverage set your career in broadcasting journalism?

A: Yes. I realized in Seoul that I had all the necessary qualifications such as theatrical talents, a reporter's instincts, and intellectualism. Connie Chung, a Chinese-American, and Ken Kashiwara, a Japanese-American, are working for the national networks. I would like to be the first Korean-American anchorwoman in a major network.

Cha said Koreans are disciplined. "They emphasize education and intellectualism. They are hard-working and family-oriented people." As for sexual equality in Korea, she said, "Some Korean women didn't want equality. Well, some American women still do. Sex was still a prohibiting factor to women's role in more challenging positions. Korean woman are sacrificing their lives for their families."

When asked whether she had anything to say to the second generation Koreans in the United States, Cha said, "A very strong sense of yourself" and "excellence."

CHAPTER 25

Words with Marshall Pihl

Hawaii is paradise on earth. Escaping from the winter of Washington for Hawaii's beautiful flowers is an incredible refreshment. At the University of Hawaii, I met Marshall Pihl, the Harvard-educated scholar on Korean literature who practically built Korean studies in the United States. He was then associate professor of Korean language and literature. He left Boston for Hawaii in 1989. He was enjoying a full-time teaching position on the beautiful island. His translation of *Collection of Contemporary Korean Short Stories* with Bruce Fulton was just published. His new book on *Pansori of Sim Chong* would be out by Harvard University Press in 1994. He passed away a few years after we met.

I interviewed Pihl at length, and the interview was published in *Modern Praxis* in 1994. In the interview, Pihl explained how he was first exposed to Korean literature, how he got the field off the ground, who his favorite Korean writers are and more. I was beyond impressed at the man's near-exhaustive knowledge of the subject.

"I went to Korea an enlisted man in 1957," he explained. "I was assigned to the public information office, Korean Military Advisory Group (KMAG). I was a feature writer. I visited many Korean military units in which American advisors were working. But I wrote more about the Korean military units than their American advisors. I met Koreans in a different culture. I found Korea's unique culture. Naturally, I met Korean corporals, *kalmegi duge*, in the Korean public information office. They spoke in broken English, and I spoke in broken Korean. After five, friendship with my equals included enjoying drinks, sometimes a lot of drinks. I came to like Korean people and their culture. Later, I enjoyed reading the works of Kim Dong-in, Hyun Jin-kon and Yom Sang-sup. They set a great example of Korean literature in the 1920s. Their works have quality and excitement. They personally had sad lives under Japanese rule, but they created a big area for literature. For example, Hyun Jin-kon was drinking himself to death, but his works ranged from outrageously funny (*Piano* and *Supervisor B and Love Letter*) to sad, extremely sad (*Hometown*) ones. The last sentence of *Hometown* is still strikingly touching to me.

"After two years in Korea, I returned to Harvard. Then, I changed my major from psychology to East Asian studies, with a specialty in Korean studies. In 1960, I was the first graduate of Korean studies at Harvard.

"How do you look at modern Korean literature?" I asked.

"I look at modern Korean literature as a capital letter U *(like the up down up swing of the letter U)*. Following the brilliant starting of Kim Dong-in, Hyun Jin-kon and Yom Sang-sup, the works of Hwang Soon-won, Kim Dong-ri and Oh Young-soo were impressive. They made a good literature in terms of craftsmanship. Hwang Soon-won is most careful in his writings; Kim Dong-ri is more complex than people think; and Oh Young-soo is very nice in all senses. They all knew the taste the Korean people liked. They were never boring. They had their own spices inside their foods, but they were not exciting.

"They were followed by the blackout of the 1940s and 1950s." The April 19, 1960 student uprising changed Korean literature. The Korean writers felt "strength." The student uprising stirred up Korean literature. The uprising toppled the Syngman Rhee government. The March 1, 1919 movement against the Japanese rule did not change the Japanese rule, but the April 19, 1960 student uprising did change the Korean society and literature. I saw Kim Seung-oak's impressive *Seoul, 1964, Winter*, which was a new up-starting point of U. He led a new generation, the Hangul generation, or the Liberation generation. Even though he did not produce meaningful works after *Seoul, 1964, Winter*, he opened new literature, totally different from his predecessors. I found Cho Se-hi's *Ball shot up by Dwarfs*, a series of short stories, 1975-1977 in this vein. In the 1980s, I met Kang Suk-kyung, Oh Jung-hi, and Kim Chi-won, three Korean woman writers; Choi Soo-chul; and Yoon Hung-gil. For example, Yoon Hung-gil uses Kim Dong-ri's techniques of using Korean shamanism or "nativism," but criticizes modern society in his *Flood*. Kim Dong-ri did not openly criticize modern society.

"I see the 1920s as the first peak and the 1980s as the second peak of U."

What makes a literary work good, and what makes it not-so-good?

"While reading the work, I often first think it is good. Then, the work starts to seem not so good as I thought it was. Something is wrong. Then, I stop reading it. Not so good works drive me out of `reading. After reading, my evaluation can be different. Good works make me think." This struck as a "You know good work when you see it" explanation, which is true enough.

"You are also an expert on classic Korean literature, Sim Chong. How did you become involved in Korean classics?"

"Well, I returned to Korea after the coursework for a field trip in 1969. Harvard stressed the classics. Harvard still prefers classic to modern literature. In my graduate work, I studied the story of *Hong Gil-dong*, translated and commented on it. There was no one who was able to teach Korean classic literature, so I learned myself."

"In Korea, I met Professor Kim Dong-wook at Yonsei University. He suggested Pansori of Sim Chong. He told me that Pansori Chun Hyang has been extensively studied, and has been translated into English, but Sim Chong has not. As you know, Sim Chong is the beautiful woman in the Korean literary works and folklore. So I accepted the very challenging work. I reviewed and analyzed one syllable to another for my doctoral dissertation. I made many questions for Professor Kim when I met him weekly. He showed me four boxes of cards made during that time. Pansori is the mixture of drama, song, narration and legend."

I next asked Pihl to comment on the current literary scene in Korea — with specific reference to the blending of literary nationalism, that is, the literature of sentiment about the country, and literary populism, which is to say anti-elitist, pro-"Common Man" writing. "Literary nationalism and literary populism cannot be mixed," he said. "Nationalism is good for Koreans' ethnic awareness. It provides an opportunity to understand who Koreans are and master their destiny. Literary nationalism has many successes. However, literary populism is based on Marxism or Leftism, and has not succeeded yet. It is not a literature yet. It is very divisive or exclusive."

Next was North Korea. "You wrote an article on North Korean literature in 1977. Have you done any follow-up studies?" I wanted him to comment on North Korea literature generally.

He had done no follow-up studies, but, as he put it, "I believe that North Korean literature is the same as before. Kim Il-sung uses literature to attempt to engineer the human soul — literature should serve the state and the Communist party. Kim Il-sung borrowed A.A. Zhdanov's words, Engineer of Human Soul for North Korean writers and artists. He was a terrible man who killed good Marxists in the 1930s and killed good literature since then in North Korea. He constantly advocated that literature must serve the state. He purged the literature and writers who did not follow his instruction. Lenin, Stalin, Mao and Kim viewed the literature as a means for the Community Party and ideology. Under Kim, there is slim chance for literature.

How does Pihl assess the globalization of Korean literature?

"I don't like to use the word 'internationalization' because it assumes the content or style of Korean literature should be changed for an international market or readership. Rather, I like to use globalization, because it means distribution or outreach of Korean literature to the world society. Translation is a key to globalization. Translators must be bi-lingual, and bi-cultural. Bruce Fulton and his wife recently translated the works of three Korean writers, *Words of Farewell*. Their translation was superb. Most translations of Korean literary works have been grammatically done, often no more than grammatical. It should be a literary translation. It should not be mechanical."

Toward that end, he said, "Translators deserve better care. Translators have been overlooked. Book reviewers often ignored the translator's skill and style. In the Yi dynasty, the translators were the *choongin*, lower class people. That tradition may still linger in modern Korea. Translators should be responsible or accountable for literary translation. If they are not responsible for literary translation, their translation must be failure.

Finally, I asked, what was causing the boom in Korean studies in the United States suddenly in the 1990s?

"The Korean population in America is rapidly growing. They will be the largest Asian population in the United States in the near future. Their children have reached college age. They pressure colleges and universities to create Korean Studies programs, and their children, now college students, pressure the university presidents to offer more courses in Korean studies. The Korean-American students at Brown went to the president, and the president promised them to offer more courses. Korean studied will be progressing from political science and economics to literature and history. It is a good progress."

Pihl spends most of his time in his office, 6:30 in the morning to 6:30 in the evening everyday. I was beyond impressed by his workmanlike scholarship. He left his wife and two college-going sons in Boston. He told me that he has 'a lot of catching up' to do, because he had been only part-time faculty since earning his doctorate degree in 1974. I presented a tape of *Samulnori* as a token of my thanks and friendship. He really appreciated my gift. I appreciate his care of Korean literature and studies as a Korean poet and writer who does not teach Korean literature or Korean studies, but teaches American Government and pubic policy.

CHAPTER 26

North Korea: A Literary View

Every Korean and Korean-American wonders when the artificial division between North and South will end and how it will happen. As I explained in Chapter 23, my own view is that U.S. troops will need to withdraw at some point, and that unification is in the long run the goal of every person who cares about Korea. But with the current regime of North Korea, the goal is beyond distant. As a matter of contemporary policy for any interested government, it makes the most sense to focus on how the balance of power is managed. We are largely powerless to force the North Korean regime to open itself and to stop abusing its own people, though we can alleviate the suffering with smart policies. We simply can't make an ideal world appear immediately the way some seem to think.

Those who supported Kim Dae-jung's so-called Sunshine Policy seem to think that the answer lies in the correct set of incentives and enticements for the North, which, in their view, the international community has not yet credibly offered. When they are (so this thinking goes), North Korea will put aside its bellicosity. I see little or no evidence for it, but the opinion is widespread and growing in South Korea.

In the meantime, North Korea's nuclear development has been making the headline news for nearly two decades now. The International Atomic Energy Agency and the United Nations have condemned North Korea's clandestine development of a nuclear arsenal of weapons of mass destruction. These weapons threaten the security of South Korea and Japan, and perhaps even the United States. North Korea's actions regularly threaten to accelerate the arms race between the two Koreas and in turn heighten old tensions and animosities between China and Japan. The United States' role in maneuvering between China and Japan and between North Korea and South Korea is increasing in difficulty and importance.

Why does North Korea act so unreasonably? What does it gain from a nuclear arsenal? Is North Korea trying to create fear and conflict intentionally in order to divert attention from domestic troubles such as the food and energy shortages?

The Geneva Accord in October 1994 opened a diplomatic relationship between the United States and North Korea. Dismantling North Korea's nuclear arsenal requires America's help in establishing light-water reactors in North Korea. North Korean harbors opened and received U.S. ships transporting crude oil. But the Geneva Accord was abandoned, because North Korea secretly developed nuclear arms. Later, the six-nation talks were initiated, but the outcome is yet to be seen.

North Korea can be likened to the "animal farm" in George Orwell's famous novel of the same name. It is a mysterious country under a personality cult, that of Kim Il-sung and his successor, Kim Jong-il. North Korea and Cuba are the last remaining hardcore Communist countries in the world. North Korea has been closed to the West. It is an unknown, mysterious country to us.

When I attempt to unveil North Korea, I do it by reviewing North Korean literature. North Korean politics and society have been analyzed almost exclusively by social scientists. But no one has seriously attempted to understand North Korea through its literature, even though there is much to learn. A people may most faithfully present ideas, thoughts, ignorance, hostility, excuses, national viewpoints and worldviews in a given country's literary works. North Korean politicians and diplomats may hide their ideas and thoughts under the name of diplomacy, but North Korean writers may not necessarily hide their inner sentiments — even when they are following the Communist party line.

Professional literature supplies knowledge and skills to its readers. Wit and experience buttress these. Yet more is needed, the whole range of human talents. And have we not been told how (oh how often) that it is the métier of the artist to give us "insight", "vision", "wisdom": a type of knowledge accessible neither through science nor common sense?

I reviewed the *Chosun Munhak* (North Korean Literature Monthly) from its January 1980 issue to January 1994 issues. The North Korean Writers' Association publishes this monthly magazine.

Each issue contains about 70 pages of poems, short stories, and critical essays. I investigated: (1) what kind of literary theories they developed; (2) how they view Western literature; and (3) the social reality and ideals they perceived and cherish in their short stories. I spent many hours in the Library of Congress in order to read *North Korean Literature*, because I could not check out the magazines.

(1) Literary Theories

What is (or are) North Korea's literary theory (or theories) guiding the country's literary works?

The North Korean government continued to indoctrinate its people with socialism until the early 1960s. It justified its initiation of the Korean War, 1950-1953, as a national liberation struggle, mobilizing all resources toward building a socialist country. Under the direction of the Communist party, literature and art were used to propagate revolutionary socialism. From the mid-1960s, writers and artists were expected to advocate the Chuche (which literally means "self-reliance") thought of Kim Il-sung. History was rewritten from the perspective of Kim's Chuche thought.

In the 1980s, North Korean literary critics started to discuss the "seed" theory, which originated with Kim Jong-il, the son of Kim Il-sung. In one of his speeches, Kim made the statement, "All great writers should have good seed in their literary works." It is a commonsensical word, but it has stirred up North Korean poets and writers. They spent the first five years of the 1980s extensively discussing the meaning of the seed theory.

One critic said, "Seed theory is searching for a balance between ideology and aesthetic sense or artistic craftsmanship." Another said, "It is the philosophic depth of the literary works." In order to settle the dispute, the North Korean Writers' Association attempted to find the seeds in their so-called classic literary works, *Blood Sea*, *Fate of a Militia Man*, *Flower-selling Maid*, *Traditional Worshipping Place*, and *Mr. Ahn Jung-keun shot Ito Hirobumi*. The seeds in their classic works are class struggle, national liberation, permanent revolution, Kim Il-sung's fight against the Japanese army and the United States army, and his victories.

In the mid-1980s, North Korean critics started to say that "literature is a study of man," which originally appeared in

Kim Jong-il's book, *On Cinema*, reported in the February 1992 issue of *Chosun Munhak*. Kim said, "Literature is a study of man. Literature should not come from an empty sky; it should come from real human life experiences." He emphasized that Kim Il-sung was the man who fought the Japanese Manchurian Army and defeated it, who fought the mighty U.S. army and defeated it, and who reconstructed the North Korean economy from the ashes of the Korean War. His speeches were made on the occasion of publishing a series of novels on the life of Kim Il-sung, his father, under the name of "Never-perishing Literature." "Literature as a study of man" includes: stories about a lovely young woman who married a disabled veteran from the Korean War; the humble man who enjoyed equality under Kim Il-sung's leadership; a teacher who could not leave her countryside school for her fiancé in a city; a worker who produced more than his assignments; a scientist who invented a new sophisticated technology in a steel mill; a prisoner of war; and an employee who produced his works ahead of schedule among many others. All these people are small Kim Il-sungs.

In 1991, the North Korean Writers' Association advocated "Our Way of Making Creative Works" modeled after the party line, "Let's Maintain our Own Socialism." They recognized the fact that the Cold War was gone, and that the USSR was dismantled, and East European communist nations were converting to free market economies. Our own style of socialism never knows defeatism, it only knows victories.

In the first four years of the 1990s, North Korean literature pursued seemingly conflicting goals: xenophobic nationalism, worshipping Kim Il-sung, Kim Jong-il and Kim Chung-sook, the elder Kim's first wife and the younger Kim's mother, and anti-U.S. imperialism, scientific and technological advancements, economic development, food production by making land reclamation projects to expand farm land and crop diversification. North Korean literature reflected what North Korea lacked: internationalism, advanced science and technology, food, new leadership, and stability. North Korea felt threatened by the outside world, and wanted to close its doors, but it also wanted economic development and technological advancements.

(2) On Western Literature

Kim Il-sung made a speech at the Asian and African Writers' conference in Pyongyang in 1980 which attacked the U.S. cultural imperialism that was penetrating all the developing nations and destroying their nationalism and traditional values. He said in his speech: "Literature is the soul of the nation and the mirror of the time. Writers are the protectors of national conscience and ideals, and guardians of the national spirit. Writers are great when they portray the national fighting spirit in their literary work. They have a noble mission before time and history." His speech was reprinted in the *Chosun Munhak* in the April 1992 issue. Kim Il-sung emphasized that the writer's mission was to protect national and traditional values from U.S. imperialism, capitalism, and that South Korea was a typical U.S. cultural colony.

One North Korean critic identified Americanism as "Yankeeism" which was again identified as: loneliness, betrayal of children against their parents, lust, emotional starvation, child abuse, homosexuality, brutality, fear, abnormal sexuality, hatred, and massacres as shown in the Korean War.

A group of North Koreans viewed Existentialism represented by Camus and Sartre as the approximation of human limitation, loneliness, insecurity, humiliation, fear and a killer of the fighting spirit of the masses, the philosophy of death. They sometimes called it "America's tragedy." They characterized Western literature as useless and destructive.

They do not understand the ambiguity of poetry. They described all Western poems as 'garbage', 'waste products', 'anti-masses', 'and/or reactionary bourgeoisie'. They were very critical of 'art for the sake of art', and claimed that so-called 'pure literature' is not useful for human welfare at all. They condemned 'naturalism', 'imagism', 'romanticism', and other literary thoughts. Poetry and novels should only serve the masses' welfare, idealism, and revolutionary romanticism.

They saw Western literature as a tool of capitalism and imperialism as they see their literature as the tool of 'socialist realism' or a party propaganda machine. They believed that literature and art should espouse progressive ideas to lead to the attainment of socialism.

The loyalty to class consciousness, which is the most essential element of socialist realism, originates from the presupposition that every artistic work reflects the ideology of an artist, and that art in a class society always has a specific class orientation. Supporters of socialist realism believe that literature and art should represent the proletariat's ideology, as all artistic works in a capitalist society inherently represent a bourgeois ideology. As Maxim Gorky put it, these requirements amount to a principle of the 'realism of people who are reconstructing and rebuilding the world' and suggests the way in which literature can contribute to their struggle for socialist development.

(3) Short Stories

North Korean writers have "clear" goals in their short stories. Some aim at praising Kim Il-sung, Kim Jong-il and Kim Chung-sook, or the Kim family. They have been portrayed as the most humanitarian, brave, and compassionate super humans. They are portrayed as being geniuses in music and military strategies, and recently in science and technology. Stories that exalt the Kim family increased in number and in intensity in 1992-1994.

The *Chosun Munhak* allocated one or two stories monthly on the Korean War in the 1980s, but that number increased to five stories in the 1990s. In these stories, the People's Army is the symbol of national security, the fighter for independence and the human willpower to resist U.S. imperialism. A story on the Pueblo incident appeared in the February 1992 issue of the *Chosun Munhak*. In that story, Kim Jong-il's brilliant military strategies and tactics, and bravery in capturing the U.S. intelligence ship, Pueblo, in the East Sea was praised. The U.S. intelligence vessel had been monitoring North Korean military movements when it was seized in Wonsan Bay on January 23, 1968, with 83 crew members, including a number of intelligence officers. They were charged by the North Korean authorities with spying.

The writer of this short story attempted to demonstrate Kim Jong-il's military knowledge and tactics which were superior over those of the United States'. He also attempted to remind his readers of the last direct confrontation between North Korea and the United States. Anti-American sentiment had been heightened in the 1990s, even though North Korea had been trying to establish diplomatic relations in the 1990s.

Short stories on rural and community development constantly appeared throughout the 1980s and the 1990s. Beautifying and glorifying nature, traditional values, people in farming improvements, the scientific farming methods, the expansion of farm land were the main thrust of their short stories. All these short stories show inequalities between cities and countryside, food shortages, and primitive farming methods. Young men in the countryside have a hard time finding brides because the latter prefer to marry urban men. A completely planned society, such as North Korea, still shows a serious widening gap between urban and rural areas.

Stories on manufacturing industries such as the textile industry and the machine industry constantly appear with stories on steel mills, electric power plants, and mining towns. They discuss leadership issues, party bureaucrats' conservative or passive attitudes, and the workers' passionate desires to innovate technology. Economy and efficiency, effectiveness, productivity, management by objectives, management by results, and management by crisis are all familiar themes in North Korean short stories too.

Science and technology, research and development have become more visible since the mid-1980s. The January 1993 issue of *Chonsun Munhak* had two stories, both of which are dedicated to the advancement of science and technology that will contribute to economic development. Science fiction was for the first time mentioned by the magazine in its August 1992 issue in order to develop people's scientific mind.

Scientists and technologists were once considered as outsiders in the Proletariat revolution. Different times dictated a different outlook on professional workers, now, they are part of the proletariat. They claim that North Korea is a professional society, so that all workers are professional proletariats. A new professional class has seemingly emerged. North Korean writers are urged to write on high-tech industries, not on the primitive technologies they dealt with before.

Reunification of Korea has appeared as a theme in North Korean short stories since 1990. The most impressive short story is "Bird"

(*Chosun Munhak*, March 1990 issue). An old ornithologist's will is to postpone the publication of his life-long research on birds because there should be one book on all the birds in the Korean Peninsula. His works were about the birds in North Korea. So he suggested that there should be one book on all the birds in North and South Korea. This story has been well received by South Korean readers. It may be a publishable piece in the Western world, if the excessive anti-U.S. sentiments could be lessened. Whenever North Korean writers write about division of Korea, they always accuse and bitterly attack the U.S. imperialists.

Another story is on one unified table tennis team from the two Koreas playing in an international tournament, "Unforgettable Night" (*Chosun Munhak*, March 1992 issue). The unified team composed of the best players from North and South Korea was impressive. They won the World Championship. The triumph of one Korean team in the international tournaments impressed North Korean writers to aspire to the nation's unification through sports. The writer still blamed the United States which divided one Korea into two.

Many stories in which characters search for Korea's unification also touch upon South Korean society where the unification-aspiring college students and professors, and other nationalists, are purged by South Korean government agencies. North Korean writers describe South Korea as a repressive and depressed 'southern half' run by "running dogs of the U.S. capitalists." Koreans in the United States and Canada frequently appeared in North Korean short stories in the 1990s. A typical story is a Korean-American visiting Pyongyang in order to establish a joint venture there, and accidentally discovering his brother from North Korea when he was separated by the Korean War. This type of story reflects many Korean-Americans' recent visits to North Korea. Some stories attempted to say that Koreans in foreign countries are disappointed with South Korea's repressive and un-nationalistic regime, and later discover the paradise of the home country, North Korea, under Kim Il-sung's great leadership.

South Koreans in Japan were depicted as corrupt, ugly, non-nationalistic, materialistic, and undesirable elements, and pro-North Koreans in Japan were all Puritan-like, nationalistic leaders. Forty percent of Koreans in Japan have ties with North Korea because their relatives live in North Korea. The *New York Times* on November 1, 1993 reported that North Korea's nuclear project has been financed by money from the Koreans in Japan. Six hundred million dollars move from Japan to North Korea annually.

Old Korean history is used for North Korean short stories. Humble men and women fighting against Japanese invasions in the 16th century are popular. Protecting the nation with courage and bravery in a crisis seem to be the objective of these stories. The nation is always defined in relation to class. A butcher and a woman, members of the lowest social class in the kingdoms, defended Pyongyang from foreigners' invasions in the stories. They have been glorified, because they have sacrificed their precious lives for the 'nation'.

* * * * *

North Korean literature promotes socialist ideology, new technology and Puritan communist culture. Kim Jong-il has been criticizing North Korean literature as lacking philosophic depth, aesthetic sense, sensitivity, and artistic craftsmanship, and thus as mundane, mechanical, repetitive, and 'distant from life'. His different theories, 'the seed theory', 'literature as a study of man', and 'Our Own Creative Works', attempted to correct weaknesses in North Korean literature. I doubt his theories have achieved what they were supposed to accomplish.

North Korean literature in the 1980s and 1990s had the same problems as the rest of North Korean reality. The economy suffered from numerous bottlenecks that lead to shortages in many areas. Transportation and power were continuously serious problems, and every year, there was renewed effort to overcome them. Railroad electrification continued, and the introduction of heavier rail cars, but all seemingly failed to overcome and get ahead of the ever increasing demands on the transport system. Power shortages have been the norm. The inability to ensure power cripples machinery and disrupts production. Hydroelectric power has been emphasized and then thermal power got attention.

North Korean writers have never written about shortages of transportation and power. They never write about shortage of food. They produce many short stories on land reclamation projects and scientific production of food. Even if they would be purged and killed, North Koreans could not complain to Kim Jong-il, because Kim Jong-il is God, and his father was father of God.

Judging from North Korean literature, North Korean society is isolated to only the thought of Kim Il-sung's Chuche. The country is deteriorating due to its economic stagnation and decline, and its loss of nearly all international allies. It shut its door, and controls the people with Chuche thought. North Korean writers have not written down any short story on the United Nations Development Project on the Tumen River Basin and the Najin-Sungbong free trade zone, opening of Mountain Kumkang for South Korean tourists for revenue, reconnection of the railroad between North and South Korea, construction and stoppage of light-water reactors after the Geneva accord for electric power by South Korea, development of Kaesong industrial complex by South Korean government and business, and enormous monetary and material assistance from South Korea to North Korea. In the 2000s, I could see only 'military first' theory or ideology in their literature.

I don't see any hope.

* * * * *

My Mt. Kumgang tour

In the summer of 2004, I climbed up Kumgangsan, or the "Diamond Mountains," part of North Korea located less than one hour by car from the South Korean border that has been opened to foreign tourists. Recently, North Korea opened the 50-foot barbed wire of the Demilitarized Zone (DMZ) for the Hyundai Kumgangsan ground tour project by bus. And so, for the past several years, tourists could access Kumgangsan by taking a ferry from Sokcho. The ferry, though, faced financial difficulties and was closed when the land route started this summer.

It was unbelievable to me that I could reach Mt. Kumgang in only an hour. It seems a ridiculously short distance to set foot in North Korea, which seemed so far away for so long, ever since the Korean War ended in 1953. The 50-foot opening in the 155-mile DMZ made the Mt. Kumgang tour inexpensive and accessible. Imagine: It has taken 50 years to remove this tiny part of the DMZ even though

South Korea has spent more than 10 years pouring humanitarian and economic aid into the North, it gained this much concession from the North. Some may praise this concession as a miracle.

There are many families separated by the DMZ who cannot exchange letters even now. They are permitted to meet at Mt. Kumgang hotels for a very limited time, staying in separate hotels.

The North Korean regime set another barbed wire boundary between tourists to Kumgang and the nearby North Korean residents. There is a nearby village of about 300 residents but they are not allowed to approach the Kumgangsan tourists. We were not allowed to take pictures of them even from inside the bus. The penalty is harsh and humiliating, according to our tour guide.

During my stay of two nights and three days, I saw the isolated village residents using primitive tools, students in uniforms, and grim, tense-looking soldiers. They were indifferent to us. We were able to meet the mountain keepers who had Kim Il-sung pins on their shirts, but were advised not to discuss any political and ideological topics with them.

The Kumgang Mountains are very rocky and beautiful. Tourists are offered various climbing excursions: I went on a four-and-a-half hour course which passes the famed Kuryong (Nine Dragons) waterfall, and another three-and-a-half-hour course which passes many rocky peaks of a million shapes. Tall pine trees had red trunks. I noticed that other hills on our bus ride to Kumgangsan were all treeless. I inferred that North Korea's energy crisis and flooding disasters made it necessary to use trees for fuel. The bald mountains must have contributed to the recent flooding disasters.

Tourists can also visit the freshwater Samilpo (Three Days) Lake, near the East Coast, for a one hour walk. They enjoy a hot spring bath with a spectacular view of the mountains.

The Mt. Kumgang tour, for two nights/three days, costs 600,000 won, or around $500. Out of this, $200 is paid to North Korea. Through the Mt. Kumgang tourism program, the North Korean government earns much-needed foreign currency in a more legitimate way than selling arms or opium (which they allegedly have done in the past).

Tourists can purchase North Korean beer, wine and hard liquors including famous snake drinks, for $15 to $30. On the first night, I went to sleep after tasting 10 different kinds of North Korean liquors!

I was angry for the divided nation and the limited opportunities for tourism under the watch of North Korean guards. On the second day, I enjoyed the Pyongyang Circus, one of the top-ranked such troupes in the world. Their presentation was superbly graceful and artistic, and ending with a slogan, "We are one!"

Yes, we speak one language, and share the same traditions and history, but we are certainly not one in ideas and thoughts, I reflected later. North Korea does not allow even letter exchanges. How could we become one?

During the first day's mountain climbing, a North Korean mountain guide admonished me when I tried to sit down at the Kim Il-sung and Kim Jong-il monuments on the mountain path.

"This is a sacred place. You should not dare to sit down there!"

How come? I wanted to say that those dictators ruined the country and starved the people.

These were monuments on the path glorifying the North Korean leaders. Some of the natural rock faces were engraved with words such as "Sovereignty," "Self Reliance," "Great Leader," and "Dear Leader." These engravings ruined the natural scenic beauty of the mountain. North Koreans don't seem to think the messages pollute the mountain's beauty. These may be comparable to the footprints of dinosaurs thousands of years later. Who knows?

The Mt. Kumgang tour has the potential to attract many nature lovers and conservationists. Similarly, the DMZ could be converted into one long 155-mile nature park. If this were accomplished, North Korea could attract many tourists and earn enough foreign currency to eradicate poverty and starvation. North Korea should be willing to offer tourists access to the natural scenic beauty free from communist propaganda, and should allow the tourists to travel freely.

The Mt. Kumgang tour program (via ground transportation) is less than one year old. Now, railroad construction to the site is underway. After this route is completed the cost will be further reduced. More people will appreciate the beauty of these rocky mountains. But more freedom for tourists is essential to attract more tourists, not just South Koreans, to visit the delicately beautiful mountains.

When we left Mt. Kumgang village, another group of South Koreans arrived to meet their separated relatives in the North. Their family reunion would be very limited and would be conducted under North Korean supervision. The visitors would not be allowed to sleep even one night in the same hotel room. Their family reunion would bring more sorrowful and painful memories to the North and the South.

No one can be certain about the next round of the family reunions. Everything hinges on the political will of the North Korean dictator.

Poem
-At Mt. Kumkang Village, North Korea

I was more comfortable in the darkness.
The black night was concealing
The poor farmer's grimace,
His primitive tools,
His barren fields,
His undernourished children,
Barbed wire between us
And the soldiers' tense eyes
Between us.

Fireflies flying in the darkness
Reminiscent of a mid-summer night's dream,
Still alive in the mountain village.

And a falling star in the darkness
Magical in an otherwise dark land.

I like the dark night.
Blinding me to the melancholy of the village
At Mt. Diamond village.

CHAPTER 27

Returning to Korea, Coming back to the U.S.

Life is Short/Autobiography as Haiku

My son set up an alarm before we went to bed. I told him, "Son, don't worry! We don't have precious things the thief aims at." My son told, "I have Mother! She is precious to me!" I realize that I have taken my wife for granted so long. I was ashamed of my statement. Then I saw my wife. Her face turned as red as an azalea flower blossomed. How beautiful the night we have at home together.

—published in the *Washington Post*, Sept. 14, 2004

In 1996, I had an opportunity to teach at the University of Seoul as a visiting professor. My mother desired my presence because she was getting old, weak and lonely in her old age. She lived with her granddaughter, my sister's daughter, who was ready to be married. Spending a few years with her through my visiting professorship was a dream come true for my mother and me.

However, after a couple of years with my mother, it was painfully difficult to say goodbye to her. So I sought a permanent job. In 1999, I was offered a permanent teaching position on the condition that I renounce my U.S. citizenship. I had no other options.

The U.S. Embassy in Seoul did not accept my explanation of why I relinquished my U.S. citizenship. As I stated then, "My job at the University of Seoul forced me to give up my citizenship." But the U.S. government did not accept such an explanation. When I reported this to the University of Seoul, they did not care. So I filed a different explanation: "Now, I want to return to the home country to finish my career at the University of Seoul and teaching Korean students is a special pleasure." Finally, the U.S. Embassy accepted my renouncement of citizenship.

I was able to make biannual trips to my home in Virginia during the summer and winter to spend time with my family. My wife visited Seoul during April of every year while I was there. I had some difficulties whenever I arrived at the Washington Dulles airport. The immigration officer inquired about the purpose of my trip. In the beginning, I told him, "I came home!" He or she must have thought I was mentally retarded, and gave me a hard time. Later, I became wise, and I answered: "In order to conduct my scholarly research projects at the Library of Congress."

My mother passed away in March of 2004. My wife respected my decision to retire at the University of Seoul in 2006. I only had a couple of years left in my teaching career. When I returned to Virginia in 2006, my wife petitioned for my permanent resident status, which, thankfully, came through in 2008.

* * * * *

Family affairs

Grandma's daughter is my mother. Grandma's sister's daughter is my aunt. Grandma's brother's son is my uncle.

What's the exact number of chon (kinship degrees) among the three individuals? I don't know the exact answer.

The exact number of chon is not important to me at all. Although they are not siblings, my mother has regarded her cousin as her own sister, and regarded her cousin as her own brother for her whole life. I have always thought of them as "Emo" (mother's sister) and "Oesuk" (mother's brother) for my whole life. Calling them as Emo and Oesuk is incorrect. But no one cares. My mother was the only offspring of my grandma, and the two were my grandma's niece and nephew. I was one of her two grandsons. The four of us, my mother, Emo, Oesuk, and I are related to each other because of my grandma who offered enormous love to me and my younger brother in her relatively short life.

My mother, though lonely by birth, had her sister and brother. When I was young, I never knew my mom was the only child of my grandma. My mom, Emo and Oesuk have maintained a beautiful relationship. I was a close observer of their triangle relationship. When one was in sorrow, the other two were always nearby to give comfort. When one was elated, the two others would quickly join the laughter. Their closeness was brought about by the fact that my mother was an only child. Most other children played with their brothers and sisters.

I joined them some years back during a farewell dinner party for my Emo's departure to her country house at Chongup, North Cholla Province. Although it was kind of a sad evening, it was unforgettable.

My uncle invited my mom and me to Emo's apartment, which she would soon vacate. Since Emo could not come to a restaurant, he chose Emo's place as the venue for the dinner. Food was delivered to the apartment. The evening may be the last gathering of the three in Seoul. All were in their eighties. They all knew their remaining years were not very many. Realizing this fact was sad and disappointing for me. The meaning of that evening is really tearful.

They cheered me. Emo and Oesuk admired my presence in Seoul. I returned to Seoul to take care of my aging mother. "It is not easy for you to come to Seoul after giving up your college teaching job and your family in the United States." I have been trying to comfort my mother, but I was always a son short of filial piety. But they cheered me up and I thanked them for their kind remarks.

My uncle brought up one old story that took place during the Japanese colonial rule. I felt as if I were looking at a black and white picture that is losing its original black and white colors. He often visited my mom in secret, because my mom was a young girl who was treated as if she were a maid at her father's house in Kwanchol-dong, Chongno, near Pagoda Park. He still remembered the address. My mother, then a young girl, attended elementary school and then high school in Seoul. My grandpa had another wife, educated in a modern school in Seoul, after abandoning his first wife, my grandma, a farm woman. A young girl lived in that house as a Cinderella or Kongj-like maid. My uncle was always cautious in approaching the residence because he might be caught by the woman of the house and thought to be an intruder. He lightly knocked on the door or window of her room next to the main door. Their encounters were brief. I first thought he came to visit my mom under the request of his aunt, my grandma.

My guess was wrong. My uncle told me that grandma could never have asked him to see my mother.

I hated my grandpa for abandoning his first wife for a modern educated woman, but my mother appreciated her father's taking care of her by giving her an education in Seoul, from elementary to the prestigious Kyonggi Girls' High School.

On the way home that night from my aunt's apartment, I found the meaning of life, and the value of my family. They lived through the hard farm life, Japanese colonial rule, liberation, Korean War, modernization, Korea's economic prosperity and current turbulent political situation. They observed and experienced many historical changes and they were always together to comfort each other. They shared both joyful and sorrowful times. That is the most precious thing in their lives. I never experienced such a beautiful relationship in my life overseas.

I don't mean to be xenophobic, but this country is beautiful because such wonderful sagas exist, as precious as a goldmine. There may be numerous such stories, as many as there are stars in the night sky.

Unfortunately, such beautiful human relationships are fading away in this country. Such a story only exists in an agrarian society. Modern society negates such relationships like it negates poetry. Science and technology downgrade poetry. Prose replaces verse.

I wonder whether I have taken care of my brother and three sisters as well as Emo and Oesuk took care of my mother. I regret to say we exist like islands in the sea. Existing is a better word than living. Islands exist.

They are isolated and separated from one another. I would like to defend my lifestyle in modern society – I'm devoted to my teaching, research and professional service on my island, but I am certain that my life is losing its human touch, and is thus meaningless.

I know what is beautiful. What is beautiful exists in the past.

Fortunately, it is kept in my treasury of memories. I don't know if my children can find a key to open this treasure box.

* * * * *

Published March 19, 2004 in the *Korea Time.*

Death of Mother

In the morning of March 7, my mother passed away.

We all feel sorrow and sadness when we lose our mothers. The mother is the closest person to her children. My mother prayed and sacrificed her life for her children. I lost my father 22 years ago. I lost my mother last week. Now, I feel I am standing in an empty space. I feel cold and lonely as I enter the Spring season. March 2004 was most cruel to me.

Every mother's death brings tears to her sons and daughters. My mother is tears. She was born in March 1919, a few days after the March 1, 1919 Independence Movement Day. Under the Japanese colonial days, she was educated at Tuksu Elementary School and Kyonggi Girls' High School, and became a schoolteacher. She married my father, another schoolteacher who later served under President Syngman Rhee. President Rhee's authoritarian personality turned my father off, and he became unemployed for half his active life after Rhee created his own political party, the Liberal Party. So my family maintained a frugal life-style. My mother did not complain about hard times she faced all her life.

My mother was a personal tutor to my brother and me and three sisters. She was the PTA president for her five children. Every dawn, she prayed for my education in the United States and well-being in the foreign land. She also prayed for her four other children. I always credited the successes I had to her prayers. I returned to Korea in 1996 to take care of her. As the first son of the family, I had an obligation to take care of her. I was fortunate to find a teaching job at the University of Seoul, and spent more than seven years with her. I have been separated from my wife and two children in the United States. My family accepted the hard choice. My mother appreciated my return, but she was ill. Parkinson's disease paralyzed her. She had a painful life in her last several years. I felt limited in my abilities in helping her. I wish that I were a medical doctor. Towards the end of her life, she could not enjoy her meals, because she could not chew or swallow.

I witnessed her last breath as I sat at her hospital bed. When she died, her face was finally peaceful. No more pain. Her body was moved to a funeral house. My friends and colleagues visited me for four days to comfort me. The warmth of friends and colleagues comforted me for the loss of my mother. They were touching my heart. Her casket was buried next to my father's grave in my mountain in Yongdong County, North Choongchong Province. My relatives, friends and church members came down to the burial site. They made me cry.

My friends and neighbors shared the sorrow from the loss of my beloved mother.

The funeral home was open for 24 hours a day. The son who lost his beloved mother needed comfort and warmth from his friends. They visited me through the night. I cannot thank them enough for the care and love they showed. I spent Sunday, Monday and Tuesday at the funeral home. In the early morning of Wednesday, my mother's casket was transported to my mountain. Those Korean friends are all special. That is what I have found again after the loss of my mother.

I am thankful to all my friends, colleagues, relatives and neighbors who shared my sorrow. It means a lot to me. I am grateful to those who share my sorrow. I am fortunate to have many compassionate people around me.

From now on, as the first son, I am going to take care of my brother and sisters. I may never take my mother's place, but as my mother did I will show endless love to them. I hope I can see my mother again in Heaven. That is what I am going to take care of for my deceased mother. I am going to find hope from the death of mother.

*I would like to share my poem, **Mother and Dove**, which I wrote 15 years ago , with The Korea Times readers. She was proud of my contributions to The Korea Times since mid-1960s.*

Mother and Dove

The dove mother embroidered as a schoolgirl
Pecked for food by my side ever since
I was old enough to observe my surroundings.
Even when the War destroyed everything
The dove survived

And pecked for peace in my childhood days.
The dove is given to the expatriate son.
The dove flew over the Pacific
Pecking mother's love in this coastal city
Enclosed by the Atlantic.
Mother is over 70 years old and
Although the son cannot hide his grey hair.
The dove is still flying in very peaceful past
Of the son and the mother.
Leaving mother's hand flying in her warmth.
To my side
The dove is praying for the son's peace.
Mother, my mother.
Dove, my dove.

* * * * *

Mother and My U.S. Citizenship

I had been waiting for my green card. It was painful for me, because I was a U.S. citizen for almost 30 years. For the last seven years I lived in my home country as a Korean citizen. I had to renounce my U.S. citizenship in order to get a job and take care of my aging and ailing mother. I was not a traitor, but I am treated as a traitor, as though I have committed treason. My story is not often heard, so it is hard to understand for those who have not been through this rather unusual situation.

My mother needed my physical presence and help. I had to be there. I also needed a way to support myself and financially help her. I had been a college professor all of my life in the U.S. The University of Seoul offered me a teaching job on the condition that I regain Korean citizenship. Dual citizenship was not acceptable in Korea in 1999.

Under those circumstances, I reluctantly gave up my U.S. citizenship. In 2006 I came back to my home in Virginia where my wife and children live. My wife petitioned for my green card, a nickname for special identification which allows non-citizens to be employed in the U.S. I received the green card recently. I was very thankful. It may be impossible for me to regain my citizenship, but at least I have this.

I renounced my U.S. citizenship with a story I submitted to the U.S. government in 1999. When I submitted my paper to the U.S. Embassy in Seoul, I had to provide the reason for my renunciation. For my first hearing, I cited the University regulation requiring all faculty members to hold Korean citizenship. Then, the U.S. Embassy denied my request, because it was not based on my own will. So for the second hearing, I wrote a fictional story: That I had found a new meaningful life in my homeland after my 30-year life in the United States. I wrote that teaching Korean students was truly meaningful, but more than that, I needed a job to take care of my mother.

I had to overcome the guilt of renouncing my citizenship with my strong desire to be with my aging mother. Forced to choose, I had to choose my mother. Not many American friends and neighbors understand my situation. This is an agonizing matter for the first-generation immigrant in this country. We all have just one mother. My mother's loving care and sacrifice for me, her son, was enormous and un-payable at any price. I could not betray her in her fading years.

In this space, I am presenting my poem, **Mother**, which I wrote after I lost my mother.

Mother,
Stood at Kimpo Airport's observation post,
Saw her son off
In June 1967,
Cried for a long time
Even long after his plane disappeared from the sky.

With a bowl of new clean water from the well
Every dawn
She prayed for her son's health and dream.

Her son waited for his mother's aerogram everyday:
The letter was filled with writing from top to bottom,

From right to left;
Each word protected him from all possible dangers.
Her prayer nurtured his mind.

In 1999, he returned to the mother land
To stay with her:
They were happy
After 30 years' separation,
But their happiness lasted only seven years.
He finally embraced her still-warm body
During her final moments in a hospital.

His crying was longer than anyone's
When her coffin went with dirt.
Mother sold pumpkins in the market during the Korean War,
And returned to Mia-dong at night:
She took the street car to Donam-dong,
And walked up the Mia Hill.
Her son waited for her on a tank
Bombed by the air attack
On top of the hill.
He could recognize her in the darkness.
He waited for her as a child,
Returning from the market.
But she waited for her life
Her son's homecoming.

Now, she finds comfort
Beside her beloved husband
In the mountain
Looking down the Kum River.
They may talk about life with their son
Under the stars and moonlight,
And discuss their son's poems,
And wish for him glorious days as a great poet.

* * * * *

And so it happened that I became an immigrant to the United States all over again. I enjoyed a good American life. When I first immigrated my mother remained in Korea, praying everyday for her son's success and happiness. Then she reached an old age and grew ill with Parkinson's disease and I came to Korea to be with her.

Citizenship is, and should be, more than a legal certificate. I am an American citizen in every sense except for the legal certificate. I love my new nation with its opportunities for abundant expression of freedom, and many other opportunities I cannot find elsewhere. I am comfortable breathing the air from the Pacific Coast to the Atlantic Coast. I love Emily Dickinson and Ernest Hemingway. I witnessed the 1960s as a young college student: the New Frontier, the Great Society, the Apollo moon-landing, long-haired hippies, the anti-war demonstrations, the human rights movements, and the environmental movements. I was a part of them.

During my two months of summer and winter vacation, I came home and edited a couple of books: *Surfacing Sadness: A Centennial of Korean-American Literature* (2003) and *Fragrance of Poetry: Korean-American Literature* (2005). As an invited poet, I read my poems at the Library of Congress to commemorate the centennial year of the first Korean immigrants' landing in Hawaii in 1903 (2003). My life is full of vitality in the United States. My heart dwells in this country.

When I lost my U.S. citizenship, it was for a larger purpose. But many of my American friends and neighbors felt that I betrayed my country. This is not true. I am the same person now as I was in 1999. I understand that the U.S. government cannot afford to be as generous about immigration policies post-9/11 compared with beforehand. But each individual has his or her own life far beyond what is defined in any law or rule. I would like to ask the U.S. Immigration Office to review my case from a humanitarian standpoint. This waiting period for me is a dreadfully long process.

I have gained permanent resident status after a long wait, and I am grateful to the U.S. government. The Asian-American History Project in Fairfax County, Virginia invited me to read my poem,

Immigrants' Dream, at the naturalization process on May 29, 2009.
With honor, I present that poem in this space:

Immigrants' Dream
—for my fellow immigrants

We came to this country with new hope,
new dream and new ambition.
We came to this country with much bigger hope,
dream and ambition.

In May 1968, I came to Seattle with $70 in my pocket.
I finished my studies, while washing dishes
and working in factories every summer.
Teaching in the fall of 1972
I found myself the" immigrant" enveloped within
The great heart of the University of Wisconsin.
Later, the enormity of the Pentagon, HUD and NASA
Might have further diminished "the immigrant".
It didn't. It raised his stature to giant dimensions.
2006 welcomed the immigrant to a new journey,
the pleasant land of retirement.

This is still an open country,
A vast country from the Pacific to the Atlantic.
This is an open country for you.
Please embrace your dream.
The sky is the limit.

You had a bold dream for a richer, affluent and prosperous life,
With great hope and greater courage
You made this new country your hearth and home.
Your dreams deserve to be fulfilled in this country of opportunity.

Returning to Korea, Coming back to the U.S.

The immigrants,
They made America Great.
The immigrants are US, the United States of America.
We are America.

Our dreams, our sweat moves this, our country, this country forward,
This world moves forward
The Depression we see today
Our children and their children will not witness tomorrow
and the day after tomorrow.
Because We, the immigrants, will move this Country forward
as in the past.

My fellow new citizens,
Let us do our very best.
God will help those who help themselves.
Let our sons and daughters see our dream
Let our sons and daughters witness
The achievement of our dreams.

The Lady of Liberty offers Her light and guidance
Her torch, Her light is the ray of hope
Sailing from the darkened sea of night

Welcome home brothers and sisters!
Welcome to our harbor
Of New Hope, New Dream and New Ambition.
Welcome fellow immigrants no longer.
Welcome my fellow Citizens.

Epilogue

I have come this far. Life is short, having passed before my very eyes as if it all occurred within a split second. I have had the honor of meeting many wonderful people during my life in America, through the countless ups and downs that I faced since my first day on American soil. My life here from a poor student to a college professor to my current citizenship predicament shows how fragile we are in between a few good moments and coming and going puzzles by fate.

In the past 40 years, I have witnessed the United States from the legacy of John F. Kennedy's New Frontier and Lyndon Johnson's Great Society Program, and an emergence of a conservative wave of thought since the 1970s, and the peak of conservative tide by the election of Ronald Reagan in the 1980s. Then there was the Clinton era in the 1990s and the neo-conservatism of George W. Bush in the early 2000s. I was a participant observer of the 1960s in which young college students stopped the Vietnam War, organized the Civil Rights movement, and the environmental movement. The 1960s was the most dynamic era in contemporary American politics. Now, I see the Obama phenomenon in 2008. The 9/11 terrorist attacks were the most tragic of incidents, and their exact impact on the United States is yet to be seen.

My nephew, Akira Kobayashi, a student at MIT, who read this manuscript, commented: "It has been a fantastic pleasure to get to know my uncle and his life. I did not know such a man existed in my family." Akira is the grandson of my uncle from Chiba, Japan, who financed my first trip from Tokyo to Seattle in May 1968. Akira's comments made my endeavor to produce "My American Memoir" meaningful. I appreciate his assistance and support of my manuscript. I also appreciate Virginia Kim's reading of my manuscript with her sister, Jennifer. Their parents were my friends in Tidewater, Virginia and comforted me during my difficult times.

As I wrote in the beginning of this book, my life is just an average Korean immigrant's one. However, all immigrants have their unusual lives. We all have our own life stories. Leaving one's home country is not easy, but challenging. This immigrant is a romanticist who strives to see challenges where others might only see a problem. I thank my wife, who endured being a poet's wife in this world of prose, especially during the last ten years of our separation due to my living with my aging mother in Seoul, Korea. I also thank my two children who spent part of their youthful lives without me. I have not been a great father to them, but I am still trying to be a decent father.

Everybody has his or her one life. I do not have any regrets for mine. From Seattle and Bloomington to a gratifying life as a college professor, poet and writer; I also worked for the Pentagon, the Department of Housing and Urban Development, and the National Aeronautics and Space Administration for three summers.

Early in my career, I could not return to Korea upon the completion of my academic pursuits, because of my political writings. But America opened itself to this foreign student who was knocking at its door. The United States is a melting pot of all races. It is a vast land. It can afford to have different ideas and thoughts. It is truly a pluralistic country. Its openness has been challenged by the September 11th tragedy, but its openness is what has made this country great.

As a teacher, I tried to imitate William J. Siffin, my mentor at Indiana University. But I confess that I never reached his level of achievements. I still thank all my students in the United States and Korea. Admirable teacher-student relationships exist in many schools and in many nations, not just in one country or two.

My life is a blessing. I still enjoy daily morning walks through a wooded forest in a neighboring park, taking a few trips abroad in Spring and Fall, reading and writing poems and essays under the lamp. I still dream of meeting the couple who housed me during my first day and night in Seattle, and Gary Capp, my summer factory friend who loved playing the saxophone, in Bloomington. I want to say thanks to them, once again.

I have visited Seattle twice, most recently in October 2007, since I left the city at the end of 1968, and tried to find the young American couple, who would no longer be young. I dedicate this poem to the couple I still want to see. I wish to repeat it here as it was placed at the end of Chapter 1, **Seattle, My First Port-of-Call.**

Seattle

The Pacific Ocean comes to the inland and makes a city an island.
Winter means rain, not snow, to the city people.
Needle leaf trees contrast with the snow-covered mountain tops
  like the Alps.
The city still has the Space Needle, which was erected
  for the commemoration of the 1962 World Fair, Boeing, and
  the University of Washington.
But I see a Korean young man working as a janitor
  at the Roosevelt Hotel in the daytime
And as a dishwasher in the Greek Village,
  a downtown restaurant at night.
He worked all summer months of 1968
  and went to Indiana University
  after earning one semester's tuition at the end of that summer.
He returned to the town after his retirement
  from a long college teaching career
And checked into the Roosevelt hotel on Pine St. and 6th St.
No one recognizes or greets him.

He was trying to find the house of a young couple
  who accommodated his first night in America on May 30, 1968,
  but failed to find it.
He remembers this city as the place where a couple warmly welcomed
  him, a poor young Korean man who came to town with small
  money and ambition in his pocket.
He may come back to the town again in order to find them
  when they are no longer a young couple.

He falls into the depth of deep sorrow in the un-seasonal autumn rain.

Let us all be from somewhere.
Let us tell each other everything we can.

Biography

Dr. Yearn Hong Choi

Yearn Hong Choi received his undergraduate degree in public administration from Yonsei University and his master's and doctorate degree in political science (public administration) from Indiana University. He taught at the University of Wisconsin, Old Dominion University, Jackson State University, and the University of Seoul. He also worked in the Office of the Secretary of Defense (1981-1983) as an assistant for environmental quality (NASPAA Fellow) before returning to Korea. He is a retired professor and chairman of the environmental policy program at the University of Seoul Graduate School of Urban Sciences, and a member of the Presidential Commission on Sustainable Development. His name is listed in *World Who Is Who and Does What in Environment and Conservation* (Geneva, Switzerland). He contributed to the *Encyclopedia of Modern Asia* (USA) on Korean environmental affairs.

His scholarly articles have appeared in *Environmental Management, Environmental Conservation, International Review of Environmental Strategies, Journal of Environmental Education, Journal of Environmental Sciences, Nuclear Plant Safety, Environmental Engineering, Water Environment and Technology, World Affairs, Journal of Public Policy and Administration, Contemporary Review, IAEA Bulletin,* and *Asian Thought and Society* among others.

His op-ed articles have also appeared in the *Los Angeles Times, Washington Post, Washington Times, Indianapolis Star, Japan Times,* and *Virginian Pilot* among other dailies. He has been a long time columnist of the *Korea Times* and the *Korea Herald,* two daily newspapers in English in Seoul.

He is the author of *Introduction to Public Administration: Essays and Research Notes* (Norfolk: Donning) and *Readings in Public and Environmental Affairs* (Lexington: Ginn Press), *Readings in Public Affairs and Administration* (Seoul: Daeyoung), *South Korea's Environmental*

Policy and Management (Seoul: Shinkwang Publishing Co. 2008) and two books on environmental politics and administration in Korean.

Mr. Yearn Hong Choi, is a poet and writer. Mr. Choi went to the United States as a graduate student at Indiana University majoring in political science/public administration. But he was an established poet in Korea as an undergraduate college student at Yonsei University. He made his literary debut through the most prestigious literary magazine, *Hyundai Munhak* (Monthly Contemporary literature magazine). "Van Gogh's An Empty Chair" was his first poem published in the magazine. "Apple" and "New Green over the Sea-line" were the second and the third poem in the magazine. Three poems published during his last two years in college made him a famed young poet. He was the first ROTC-commissioned second lieutenant in the Korean army (1963-1965). After two years of military duty, he went to Yonsei University Graduate School and received his master's degree in public administration (1967). Then, he went to the University of the Philippines Graduate School of Public Administration as a SEATO scholar. During his one year stay in Manila, he published his poems in the *Manila Chronicle*. After one year at Manila, he went to Indiana University.

He published his poems such as, "To the Flowers of Indiana" and "America" in the *Indiana Daily* and *Nostalgia*. *Nostaligia* was an underground newspaper popular in the 1960s, with coverage of anti-Vietnam War activities and environmental protection issues as-well-as the civil rights movement. He was involved in American politics as the foreign students' representative at Indiana University. Before he left Indiana University for his first teaching job at the University of Wisconsin, he had his poetry-art ensemble at Indiana University Union Building's North Lounge for one month. His exhibit drew great attention not only from the local newspapers, but also from the Associated Press and United Press International. A Korean student's poetry was popular on Indiana University campus.

When he started his teaching career at the University of Wisconsin, he became the literary leader of the Korean-American community. He was the co-editor of the first Korean-American anthology, *Horizon,* published in Los Angeles and the editor of the

Korean-American Poetry. At the same time, he became a writer against South Korean authoritarian regime in the 1970s. He wrote to President Park Chung-hee not to kill poet Kim Chi-ha. He could not return to Korea for his political writings.

He continued writing his poems in Korean and translated them into English. He published them in the *Korea Times* and the *Korea Herald*, two newspapers in English in Seoul. His poems were read by a Fulbright Scholar from Espirito Santo University in Brazil at Georgetown University, and translated into Portuguese and published in Brazil in the mid-1970s.

He became a naturalized citizen of the United States after his son was born in 1976 and before his daughter was born in 1978. He continued publishing his poems in the United States and in Korea in the 1970s and the 1980s. His leadership in the Korean-American literary community was later evidenced by his editorship of *Surfacing Sadness: A Centennial of Korean-American Literature* (2003), *Fragrance of Poetry: Korean-American Literature* (2005), and *An Empty House: Korean-American Poetry* (2008). His poetry books are six, including *Autumn Vocabularies* (Writers' Group, Calcutta, 1990) and *Moon of New York* (PublishAmerica, Baltimore, 2008). He returned to Korea in order to be with his aging mother in 1999 on the condition that he renounced his US citizenship in order to get a teaching job at the University of Seoul. He retired from teaching in 2006, and returned to the United States. He is a permanent resident of the United States.

His mailing address: Dr. Yearn Choi, 7820 Preakness Lane, Fairfax Station, VA 22039 703-690-0331, 703-627-6711.

www.ingramcontent.com/pod-product-compliance
Lightning Source LLC
Chambersburg PA
CBHW062200080426
42734CB00010B/1757